WOMEN
WHO WALK

WOMEN
WHO WALK

How 20 Women from 16 Countries
Came to Live in Portugal

Louise Ross

Moyhill Publishing

First Published in 2018
ISBN 978-1905597-888.

A CIP catalogue record for this book is available
from the British Library.

Cover design by Michael Hultén, Graphic Designer
Cover Art by Christina Hultén,
Christina's Charity Art *www.facebook.com/art4dogs*

Design and typesetting by *Moyhill* Publishing.

Moyhill Publishing,
1965 Davenport House, 261 Bolton Rd, Bury, Gtr. Manchester BL8 2NZ. UK

To the women whose voices echo in these stories…

I spent half my life traveling in foreign places. I've only lately come to see that incessant wandering as an outer expression of my inner journey.

From the travel memoir *Conundrum,*
by Jan Morris

The movement of people is as old as man, there is nothing new about it and it has always been linked to the same thing: the failure of where you are to provide you with an opportunity and so you move somewhere else.

Nana Addo, President of Ghana,
in an address to Emmanuel Macron,
President of France

Contents

Introduction

I'd read that asking 'where are you from?' often means: 'why are you here?' or, 'how did you come to be here?' Since I've been living in Portugal, and because I have been very active in the social organization *International Women in Portugal* (IWP), these enquiries loom large in my initial interactions with others.

I'm also one of those curious people who like to know where others are from, including the journey they took that caused them to be where they are now. That inquisitiveness dates back to my childhood when the only means in the 1960s of satisfying curiosity was the encyclopedia or my father, who I held to be a fountain of wisdom. "Who are the Gypsies and where are they from?" I once asked. He told me they were from Egypt, which is why they were known as Gypsies, explaining the derivation of the name Gypsies from Egyptians. That seemed plausible, though I could tell Dad was just telling me the accepted story of the time so I'd stop pestering him. The Romani or Roma or Travellers (as they're now known) continued to captivate my interest. No one seemed to really know who they were and from where they'd originated.

Thirty years later, I read that by studying the etymology of common words used by the Roma, linguists were able to deduce that they were originally from Northern India. From there a hypothesis evolved that at some point between the 6th and 11th centuries a group of Indians walked out of India and into mid-west Asia and Egypt (the story my father shared was partially correct) and then into Europe. The speculated reasons for their leaving included persecution for their religious beliefs or the possibility that they had certain unique and highly valued skills that they traded for gold in other lands. This is interesting, since it ventures to explore the origins of a people who wandered far from their homeland, and the *why* inherent in their leaving.

What does compel someone to leave their country of origin, which is the story before their departure? And then what happens to them on their journey to the new place, which is the story of getting from one place to another? And what causes them to finally land somewhere and decide to stay, if not for the rest of their lives, then for an extended period?

Since living abroad, for 33 years now, people have asked me, "Why did you leave Australia?" I don't have a simple answer. In fact, it feels as though the reasons have become more complex as I've aged and continued to stay abroad rather than return. Australia was known as the "Lucky Country," the country people wanted to move to, and still want to move to from all corners of the world due to its economic health, opportunities for a better quality of life and its geographic beauty. So why leave!? Actually it's much easier to ask others the questions we have difficulty resolving ourselves. In listening to their stories, we often find reassuring shared experiences that shed light on the grey areas of our life. And there was no better place to do that than within the community of international women in Portugal.

I moved to Portugal in 2014 having visited half a dozen times during the two years prior. In 2012, Lisbon appeared to be really suffering from the global financial crisis and the austerity measures imposed by Troika. Magnificent old buildings were boarded up, roads were in disrepair and much of the city was in need of maintenance. Portugal's former glory days as a wealthy, colonizing European capital were long gone. The city had an air of a crumbling Havana.

Along *The Linha* – the coastal train line running between Lisbon and Cascais – it was a different scene of surf beaches and a laid-back beach culture enveloped by a salty sea breeze and sea-weedy smells. The atmosphere evoked in me happy childhood memories of long, lazy days at the summer beach house in Australia where family gathered and to where my parents had retired. Before moving to Portugal, I'd lived for many years at the foothills of the Rocky Mountains in Colorado. In my 20s, I'd gone there to study, adapting to the land-locked geography, high-altitude climate, and the fitness and outdoors culture. Despite making a life and a home in the U.S. for 27 years, I missed the lifestyle that comes from being near the ocean. And that was just one of many good reasons for moving to Portugal.

My new home in São João do Estoril overlooks the Atlantic with sand and beach at my doorstep. Upon arriving, and in order to acclimatize to life in the western-most country of Europe, I enrolled in a nearby language school to learn Portuguese. I also joined IWP, a social organization created in 1990 by a group of expatriate women with a mission to help newcomers "feel at home in this beautiful country." What a sanity-saving decision that was. True to their mission, I did indeed quickly feel at home in this beautiful country with its Russian-sounding language and customs that are not, as some naïvely think, similar to neighboring Spain! In fact, one needs a totally different manual in order to navigate Portuguese culture and IWP offered help via its network of 350-plus members, women who were in the know and who were happy to share their wisdom.

In an effort to casually rub shoulders with these women, I began by participating in a weekly Friday activity, the Sintra Walk. Hiking elbow-to-elbow in scenic natural environs, I discovered, is a great vehicle for soliciting good conversation and referrals. On my initial hikes, I managed to collect names and contact details of an accountant, a dentist, a dermatologist, an osteopath and the best place to get a haircut and a mani-pedi. Plus, advice on dealing with SEF, the Portuguese immigration office: "with great patience for the slow and frustrating paperwork-heavy bureaucracy" was the uniform feedback.

Beyond the tips and tricks on living in this beautiful country, my hiking mates shared stories of where they were from, where they'd been and how they came to live in Portugal. I was hearing stories the caliber of which caused me to take stock of just how stimulating it was to be mingling with a group of worldly, educated, multi-lingual, well traveled, intrepid women, the likes of whom I'd not encountered in such numbers during my previous life. The collective wisdom of the IWP women, and other expatriate women whom I also met, needed to be recorded for posterity, I concluded. Their fascinating accounts represented more than 44 different countries – a mini United Nations – and their experiences straddled two centuries and the massive global changes that have taken place during that time.

Yet documenting the story of every interesting woman I encountered was impossible. There were simply too many. Thinking about what I wanted to explore in an anthology of women's stories for a standard size book, I came back to the following three questions: What does compel someone to leave their country of origin? And what happens to them on their journey to the new place? And then what causes them to finally land somewhere (in this instance, Portugal) and decide to stay, if not for the rest of their lives, then for an extended period?

Like me, the women I was meeting had left their countries of origin for varied reasons, but I should clarify, the women I eventually interviewed are representative of a fortunate group. None is a refugee who had to flee her country due to war, persecution, famine or natural disaster nor is she a migrant who has moved country-to-country to find work and with it better living conditions. The 20 women have come from or grown into the comfortable middle-to-upper-middle classes. They've had access to education, enjoyed a life of relative economic stability, travel and adventure and personal agency, all of which granted them opportunities and freedom to create the kind of lives their mothers and grandmothers might only have dreamed of.

They are by definition either expatriates: "*A person temporarily or permanently residing in a country other than their native country;*" the term "expatriate" is also used for retirees and others who have chosen to live outside their native country; or immigrants: "*a person who comes to a country to take up permanent residence.*" (Wikipedia)

Three years and 26 interviews later, edited down to 20 for this book, I have learned an enormous amount, in fact, this project has been edifying. Documenting the stories of my interviewees gave me the chance to do some recreational study, and a bit of armchair travel. For instance, with each story there were names and places that I needed to research in order to find the correct spelling and perhaps the geographic location. Places like Gujarit, where the people are known as India's entrepreneurs, borders Rajasthan to the north and Pakistan to the west and Rabaul, on the island of New Britain, is about 60 kilometers east of the island of New Guinea.

There were specialized fields of study or work that either the interviewee or their parent had engaged in, things that I had no clue about, but which I needed to understand in order to document the information correctly. I found myself reading about the effects of pollutants on the development of sea urchin larvae; why there's a basin in the Alboran Sea near Gibraltar; the European Organization for Nuclear Research in Geneva where physicists probe the fundamental structure of the universe; the small and highly specialized world of conservation and art restoration; and the origins of red-nose clown doctoring!

Three of the interviewees either grew up in or lived in war-torn countries with complex political situations that I needed to have some grasp of in order to accurately write up their stories. On Wikipedia I read about the Lebanese civil war, following links to many articles, digging deeper into the political and religious history of this complicated area of the Middle East. Likewise, researching the proxy war in Nicaragua led by the Sandinista National Liberation Front against the U.S. backed Contras was an ordeal of dense online reading, as was online research on the colonial wars in Angola and Mozambique and Africa's fight for independence from Portugal.

On a lighter note, the father of one of the interviewees was adopted with no way to trace his family of origin. In a tangential conversation about this, I encouraged Rosemary to do an ancestry search via DNA analysis. Ironically, I was the one that did the test out of curiosity. I learned that my genetic heritage is 18 percent western European, which is where I live now!

Before I even began the interviews, which led to the kind of research I mention above, I was excited by this project. However, I needed to run the idea by someone I trusted. I pitched the idea to a journalist friend, and occasional Sintra hiker, Pat Westheimer, an American who lived in Cascais for 25 years. Pat, who was living with cancer and who sadly died in 2016, was aware that this book idea evolved out of my conversations with some of the hikers and immediately she proposed the working title: *Women Who Walk*. I liked this! It encapsulated pertinent metaphors such as the most literal, and evoked images of women moving forward with direction, empowered women, women of strength, women with freedom to move, and so on. The title stuck. Still, getting started was daunting as living in Portugal, with all its wonderful cultural distractions, was even more exciting. And then I had an accident.

On the way to an appointment with my osteopath (the one recommended to me on an early Sintra Walk), the rubber sole of my shoes caught on the marble steps in the entryway to my apartment building. I first rolled my right ankle, and then trying to catch myself from falling, I rolled the left ankle landing on the cobbled pavement below. Fortunately, I was able to call my Portuguese neighbor from my cell phone and he instantly appeared, offering to drive me to my existing appointment. My osteopath thought it very funny that I'd sprained, not one, but both ankles! In between chuckles of disbelief, he gave me a great treatment that helped contain the swelling, and his advice: "Stay off your feet for at least two weeks."

At home, I elevated my ankles, alternatively encasing them with frozen bags of peas and applying arnica cream rubs. Friends dropped by to offer help, staying for a while to keep me company. One of those friends, Camilla, a Sintra hiker, chatted away comfortably which encouraged me to ask her questions and suddenly she was sharing stories that inspired me to pull out my iPhone and with her permission, record her talking about her journey from Sweden to Brazil, to various European countries, and eventually to a life in Portugal. This was the beginning. Unable to walk, beyond a shuffle aided by crutches, there were no excuses, it was time to begin *Women Who Walk*.

How I went about the project is simple. It started with that very organic interview with Camilla, and in fact the logistics continued to evolve organically. That said, I was conscious that I wanted a collection of stories from women who were a diverse sample of the 44 different countries represented by the membership of say, IWP. In other words, I wanted to avoid all interviewees being of the same nationality. I managed this to a degree with 20 women, born in 16 different countries.

The diversity extended to include an age range of 40-to-75 with an average age of early-50s. Eleven women are married, two are partnered, one is widowed, and six are single. Ten of the women have children. Eleven have advanced degrees. And one of the women most certainly would have pursued higher education, but she was denied the opportunity.

A reaction I heard from several women that I had asked to participate surprised me. It went something like this, "But my life is not interesting, there are other women here with far more interesting stories to tell." Despite their self-effacing comments, I encouraged them to be a part of this project. I think readers will agree with me that there is nothing boring about what any of the interviewees share. Actually, I find it unsettling that women tend to discount their lives as "less than" or "not as important". "Take pride in your strength and uniqueness; no one else can walk your epic journey for you," as a teacher of mine once said.

We all have experiences that distinguish us and to the extent that women give up the opportunity to speak about their journeys in depth, the legacy of the female chronicle will remain comparatively underrepresented. Women's lives matter and in that regard, I am honored to have facilitated the telling of the oral histories that make up *Women Who Walk,* who as a group, have traveled the world arriving in Portugal at different times over the last 30 years. If the global movements of the 20 women were depicted pictorially, we'd see a tangled web of crisscrossing lines converging at the most western point of Europe. Ironically, in the 15th century it was from this point that the great Portuguese seafarers set off in their caravel to discover the world, and now the world is discovering Portugal.

After recording each interview on my iPhone, I transcribed the conversations and in some cases distilled 10,000-plus words down to approximately 2,900, the average length of each story. Seven of the women spoke English as a second or third language and thus their unique vernacular has been partially eclipsed as I edited their stories more rigorously for clarity. Each woman approved her edited story and granted permission for it to be printed. Several women requested anonymity, choosing a pseudonym to accompany their stories. And a number of women asked me if I would include my own story. I have.

I am enormously grateful to all the women who agreed to talk with me about their families of origin, their early childhood experiences, education and subsequent careers, significant life events, their travels and adventures. And without me specifically asking, each interviewee, simply by telling her story, inadvertently answered the three questions I sought to explore. Therefore I have not written an epilogue; I did not want to consolidate what is already uniquely inferred in each narrative. However, by way of providing an ending, I asked Alison Collis, a psychotherapist from the U.K. who practices in Lisbon where she works with expatriates, global nomads, and adult third culture kids to write an Afterword.

Communicated honestly and openly, sometimes with humor, sometimes through tears filled with painful memories, the personal journeys documented in *Women Who Walk* tell tales of world travel and cultural immersion as a form of higher education, a vehicle for personal growth and expanded awareness of self and others, and an instrument also for greater understanding and appreciation of the differences that today too often separate us. My hope is that readers will find these shared experiences uplifting, exciting, poignant, and inspirational, a reassuring reflection of their own journey.

And finally, thinking about what I learned as the interviewer gathering the stories for this project, the following reflection from Barack Obama came to mind:

"I learned that if you listen hard enough, everybody's got a sacred story, an organizing story of who they are and what their place in the world is. And they're willing to share it with you if they feel as if you actually care about it. And that ends up being the glue around which relationships are formed, and trust is formed, and communities are formed. And ultimately that's the glue around which democracies work."

Dalia Mansour

Introducing Dalia

You can't miss Dalia. The girl is a live wire with big positive energy, and boy, can she project her voice while simultaneously talking so fast it's hard to keep up! Her wide smile is as dazzling as her maroon-red, corkscrew curly hair that bobs about uncontrollably when she doesn't tie it down, which generally she does. For her last birthday, I gave Dalia a DVD, a documentary simply titled *IRIS*. Featuring New York fashion icon, Iris Apfel, a nonagenarian with a unique, exuberant and colorful sense of style, I thought Dalia might enjoy it because to me, she's a young Iris-in-the-making. Plus, the promotional write-up included this one-liner: "A story about creativity and how a soaring free spirit continues to inspire."

In her words

I have vivid memories from my childhood of no electrical power at home. Bombings. And with my mother rushing between bombings to get my baby brother to his pediatric appointments.

I was born in Beirut, Lebanon in 1971 just before the civil war broke out. We lived in Ras Beirut, a middle class neighborhood of mixed religious groups: Muslim, Christians, Druze and seculars. We were surrounded by embassies, ambassadorial residences and international organizations, including the Goethe Institute, the British Council (my family was a member of both), the Lebanese American University, the American University of Beirut, the International College of Beirut, and there was a UNESCO office right opposite our house. I had dreams of one day working for the UN.

The conflict started in Beirut in the spring of 1975 when an altercation between members of the Palestinian Liberation Organization (PLO) and a Lebanese militia resulted in the death of a member of the PLO. This was followed by a revenge drive-by-shooting aimed at assassinating the leader of the Lebanese militia group, but instead, four young Lebanese civilians were killed. The militia retaliated, ambushing a bus filled with PLO, and Lebanese supporters of the PLO, killing all passengers. The chaos escalated. On December 6, the Lebanese militia set up roadblocks in certain neighborhoods and the PLO set up roadblocks in other neighborhoods, with both parties killing assumed enemies as they tried to pass through the roadblocks. The event was known as Black Saturday. The cycle of revenge and retaliation divided Beirut and Lebanon, creating Muslim and Christian neighborhoods, towns, and regions. Our neighborhood, Ras Beirut, was neutral.

Though my family is Muslim, I went to a U.S. affiliated private school as the public school system was collapsing due to the war. The private school system ran on fees, which meant a good education was available to those who could afford to pay for it, but when there was active fighting I didn't go to school. In the earlier years of the conflict, to ensure that kids didn't get too far behind in subjects such as mathematics, lessons were available on TV (when there was power), and my grandmother, who lived with us, would supervise.

During the war, Lebanon wasn't isolated from the rest of the world nor did the fighting deter people from having a social life. There were outings, parties, graduations, and weddings. We had access to current pop culture from Europe and the U.S. and news of what was going on in the world. Our lives were just very contained. We traveled very little, a few small trips within Lebanon, and then in the early '80s we went to Cyprus for a brief and fun holiday. Right around the time that Lebanon's civil war began, a military coup had also occurred on Cyprus. The initial aim was to unite the island with Greece, but Turkish troops invaded the Island to protect the rights of the Turkish Cypriotes and they subsequently divided the island. By the time we arrived for our family holiday, Cyprus, like Lebanon, was divided: the Greek Cypriotes on one side and the Turkish Cypriotes on the other. As a 10 year old, I thought "Oh, okay, religious division must be normal."

Sometime in 1982, after our trip to Cyprus, the Israeli Defense Force (IDF) invaded southern Lebanon. The Palestinian Liberation Organization (PLO) was operating on the border of Southern Lebanon and Israel, engaging in repeated attacks and counter-attacks with the IDF. The IDF in attempting to push back pockets of PLO militia invaded Lebanon and advanced on Beirut, locking down the city in a siege that lasted several weeks.

During this period we lived on tinned food and we rationed our water. The bombing was non-stop and the air strikes were intense. It was a hard time, not just because Beirut was being destroyed, but also, we feared we would be killed. Eventually that chapter concluded when a deal was struck by the "Powers That Be" and the arrival of the U.S. Marines to oversee the withdrawal of the PLO from Lebanon.

In the spring of 1989, things shifted again with conflict escalating across the country. The Lebanese military, which had weakened over the years with secular divisiveness, sought sovereignty. It was my last year of high school and there was a lot of Lebanese pride and an undeniable sense of unity. We kept on with our lives.

The war created pockets of interruptions where one neighborhood or region might be relatively quiet and in another, street fights and tensions raged. Regardless, to me, my teen years were normal: I was a big pop-culture and MTV fan – Duran Duran, George Michael – and I wore Madonna-signature fingerless gloves, and the boho fashions I saw on the streets and on fashion TV. The car bombs, impromptu clashes, and neighbors sharing generators and water delivery services were just part of that normal.

We were one of the few families in our extended circle that had not lost a family member or close friends to the war, which really was a miracle. Over 150,000 Lebanese died between 1975 and 1990 and over a quarter of the population was displaced, so our family was extremely lucky. In fact, my father continued to work in Beirut throughout the war. He had a good job and he kept at it. But as my parents began to contemplate the kind of future that lay ahead for my brother and me the reality was that Lebanon and the pervasive instability simply could not offer us a future.

War kills your capacity to plan for the future. You cannot plan, well that's not entirely true, where the planning focus goes is not to the future but to your immediate resources: do we have food, water, and are we safe today?

War also crushes dreams.

I knew my parents had dreams. They had grown up during the post WWII glory days of Lebanon when Beirut was the *"Switzerland of the Middle East."* Our small country had beach clubs and restaurants all along the coast, a marina, a casino, and ski resorts in the mountains. We had a unique cuisine identifiable by its Turkish and French influences (due to the control of Lebanon by both these countries) and our own unique Mediterranean flavors. At that time all this was unprecedented in the Middle East. This was the Lebanon my parents knew. When they began their careers in banking, they had active social lives and aspirations. By the time I, and then my brother were born, everything began to unravel. The war destroyed their city and their dreams.

By the early 1990s the war was coming to an end. My parents were thinking about emigrating. Initially they considered Australia. We applied. However Australian immigration was accepting applications from people with technical skills not banking professionals like my parents. Canada was offering opportunities, in particular Quebec, but you needed French. My mother and brother were fluent in both French and English but my father and I only spoke English as our second language. And then we learned that the Maritimes or Eastern provinces of Canada were open to Lebanese immigrants. We applied and Canada accepted us! In 1995 we landed in Halifax. Both my parents seemed exhausted, as though something in them had died with the war.

Very soon after we were settled, my brother and I were attending university in Ottawa. It was a new and exciting beginning for us. I had completed my first undergrad degree in biology while in Lebanon and my intention was to go to medical school. By the time we arrived in Canada the Brundtland Report on sustainability had come out and *Environmentalism* was the '90s new sexy. One night my brother and I were looking at university booklets and with my science credits, I decided to switch gears and do an honors program in Environmental Science. This decision set me on a vocational path in Canada's public service. During the early years of my career, I traveled extensively within Canada on a consultation project, meeting with different producer groups. It was a great experience, coming from war-torn Beirut, to go out into the fields, and visit dairy farm operations as well as beef and swine feed lots.

In 2002 I went to a United Nations meeting in New York, I was a supporting officer with the Canadian delegation. It took me right back to my neighborhood in Ras Beirut when we lived across the road from the UNESCO offices. I felt this enormous sense of pride participating in those meetings. It was not that long after 9-11 and entering the U.S. with *Lebanon* as "place of birth" in my Canadian passport was a bit edgy. Nevertheless, the questions at border control were simple: When was the last time you were there? Do you still have family living there?

I lived at home with my parents until I was about 30, and may well have continued to live at home until I married – this is the Middle Eastern tradition. Except I wasn't contemplating marriage as my career took precedence. Around this time, I was active in a chat group with Lebanese nationals living all around the world, including Canada. I met a guy through the group and we ended up having a long-distance relationship for about a year and a half. His family was in Montreal, but he ended up moving to Paris for work.

I had always thought that my match would be a Lebanese guy, someone who understood the food, the culture, the songs, and the history of my country of origin. I visited Paris several times during our relationship. I hadn't been to France before and on those visits I was aware of the influence French culture has had on Lebanese culture especially with the street names and architecture. My guy was Christian Lebanese and really interesting, but unfortunately the relationship didn't last. His parents did not approve of me due to our religious differences. He respected his parents, and we broke up.

The experience encouraged me to move away from organized religion to a more spiritual viewpoint with a foundation in kindness, humility and compassion, values my grandmother had taught me. And I also wanted to start living my life on my terms. The timing was right to move out of my parents' house. With just my desk, computer, clothes, CDs, books and my mattress, I moved into a small downtown apartment of my own. I did not discuss my decision with my parents. I knew they would disapprove, and besides, we never had the kind of open familial communication that would have allowed for such a discussion.

On the day of my move, my father wouldn't speak to me, and in fact, that was the beginning of the end of our relationship. I think his pride was so hurt by my leaving his house that he was unable to see things from my perspective, which is that I was ready to stand on my own feet and be my own person. It took me a while to adjust to being estranged from my parents. As a good Middle Eastern girl, to not have a relationship with your parents is unusual. Knowing that I hadn't done anything wrong helped me move on. And I did and still do have a very close relationship with my brother, his wife and my nephew. They're all the family I need.

From the time I arrived in Canada, I thought of myself as Lebanese-Canadian. I don't totally identify with Lebanese culture as I've lived 20-plus years in Canada, but having lived through the chaos of Lebanon's civil war, I cannot give up on my country of origin. I've always been patriotic and I love my Lebanese heritage.

Ironically, my maternal grandmother was Turkish and her extended family were Syrian by marriage. Under the Ottoman Empire the borders between Lebanon and Syria were fluid in the early 1900s. My grandmother had grown up in Istanbul as a Khanum, an aristocrat. Her family moved to Damascus, Syria and eventually to Beirut where she was introduced to my grandfather, a well-off Lebanese merchant. My mother is Lebanese, born in Beirut, but she has a prominent Syrian accent as her mother spoke to her in Turkish with a Syrian accent. Whereas my uncle has a Beiruti accent by virtue of his interactions with my grandfather, and my father is Lebanese and has a Beiruti accent. So my childhood was nuanced with the Lebanese, Syrian and Turkish languages.

I've been back to Lebanon only twice. Once in 1999, when I returned for a summer vacation while still at university, and then in 2004 when I met up with friends in Beirut. We visited places I'd never been to. The country was no longer divided and there were no longer risks to our safety.

The social scene was hopping with beach clubs, nightclubs, and endless options for a memorable summer vacation. It was obvious a few days into my stay that Lebanon was coming back to life. However, being in Lebanon is like being at the top of a mountain: the view is spectacular, but that mountain is a volcano that could erupt at any time.

The following summer in Ottawa, I was out with my girl-friends when I met the man I would eventually marry, a non-Lebanese Canadian. About a year later, we moved in together. It felt right as we have a lot in common, including our careers in public service.

In 2013, Ottawa's public service sector went through huge cuts and an enormous number of people were laid off. Fortunately, our jobs were safe. However, it caused us to think "what if?" My partner explored other job possibilities, expressing an interest in an international organization in Portugal. He applied, and a couple of months later we got the exciting news that the job was his. Before he accepted the offer, we talked about the big life change it would be for the both of us. I had some legitimate reservations: I'd be leaving behind a social network of dear friends and colleagues who'd contributed to my success as an immigrant by never treating me as an outsider; I'd miss spending precious time with my nephew; and I'd be leaving a very successful career that I'd built up over 14 years and moving to a country and city where we didn't speak the language and where I wasn't going to be able to work.

Under Canadian law our living-together relationship was considered "common law," but entering Portugal as a common law partner meant nothing to the Portuguese authorities. In other words, I had no status other than as a "visitor," which meant I'd have to leave the EU every three months minus one day. Through his employer, my partner would have benefits but I would not have access to those benefits, such as health care.

After meetings and phone calls, and one memorable conversation with a Portuguese authority that included the comment, "Senhora, in Portugal you're either married or widowed," we got married. We tied the knot at the city hall in Ottawa with two witnesses and our joke is that Portugal made us! Despite having reservations about the move, I felt ready to embrace this opportunity. I had no work-life balance in Ottawa. I'd allowed my career to consume and define me and I needed to find balance again for the sake of my health and wellbeing.

We've been in Lisbon almost three years. It's been an adjustment. I kept asking myself, "Who am I now that I'm not a public servant?" With time on my hands, I took on the role of managing our lives. I've also enjoyed tutoring, something I'm familiar with as I was a math, science and English tutor while at university in Beirut, but now I'm pursuing certification so I can tutor English here professionally.

Our friends in Canada ask us how we're living with the uncertainty of not having a permanent contract. My response is that I think we can live with not knowing where and what's next, particularly while my partner is happy doing what he's doing.

On my end, I'm not ready to let go of the great friendships we've made and this blessed new life we have. Living in Lisbon

I've discovered that I have this practicality and adaptability that evolved out of the challenges we experienced in Beirut during the war. As an example, last winter we lost power in our apartment and my partner was like, "Argh, what do we do?" I found some candles, lit them, and said, "Babe we're going to play board games, coz that's what you do at times like this!"

Where is she now?

Dalia and her husband took an extended six-week vacation this summer, a car trip through 10 European countries. Her husband is back at work under his extended contract and Dalia is enjoying the demands of tutoring 5 students, volunteering with the theater group *Lisbon Players,* while also discovering Lisbon, which she documents in her written and photographic blog, and she maintains a very active social life.

Audrey Willet

Introducing Audrey

When listening to Audrey speak, her Scottish lilt is only slightly apparent. It's more obvious with some words or certain phrases, and then it's a pleasure to hear. An unassuming, gentle and diplomatic woman, she's nevertheless a very keen outdoorswoman who enjoys her sports. We scheduled our interview around her tennis lessons, which she's still attending despite tennis elbow that was visibly bandaged on the day we met. I've only recently come to know Audrey, after discovering that she'd lived in the Middle East and visited areas with historic significance that have since been destroyed due to the various wars in the region. I was curious to hear of her experiences seeing these antiquities. One day we met for lunch and she showed me photos of places in Syria, extraordinary artifacts that have since disappeared. I thought her so lucky to have had the opportunity to see landscapes of such beauty, noting that her many pictures hold even greater value now that much of what she recorded has turned to dust.

In her words

I remember as a child visiting my paternal grandparents on occasion, where in the effort to keep my brother and me occupied, we were given a cardboard box of old photos to rifle through. Some were of my father's childhood in India: the beautiful house in which he'd spent the first seven years of his life; Dad spending summers in Darjeeling near the Himalayas; Dad with his Ayah, his Indian nanny; and pictures of my grandfather on a tiger hunt. The images were incredibly exotic and they made a big impression on me.

My father's father was the manager of a tea plantation in Guwahati, Assam near Bangladesh in the north of India. There were six children and at age 7, my father was sent to boarding school back in Scotland. He sailed from India with one of his brothers and a chaperone. Upon arrival he was picked up by his grandmother whom he'd never met, and taken to school and from then on he spent his school holidays with his grandmother and maiden aunt. He never returned to India. Just after World War II, when the British Raj fell, my father's parents returned to Scotland, by which stage my father hadn't seen his father or mother for about three years.

In comparison, my mother's mother, who was born and lived in Edinburgh, was a Gaelic speaker and the center of family life, and my grandfather, an extremely learned man, spoke Greek and Latin. My maternal grandfather would probably have gone on to be a scholar, but he needed to earn a living. My mother was very bright, and because my grandparents highly valued education, they managed to pay for her to go to private school. She then trained to be a teacher, eventually becoming a headmistress. Though it was never specifically verbalized, I think education was always considered important in my family, that and a strong work ethic.

We were a typical 1970s family, caravanning around Scotland during the holidays. Though I guess my first seven years were somewhat unconventional as we lived in the hotel that my father managed. We had an apartment above the copper still – the bar – my parents, younger brother, the two dogs and me. My brother and I would wander into the kitchen – sometimes meals were delivered to our apartment – or we'd sit at reception, and if we were well behaved one of the staff in the Lounge Bar might give us a Coca-Cola. Our friends were the people who worked at the hotel, and our gardens were the hotel gardens.

We moved out when my parents bought our family home and then I moved out when I went to Edinburgh University at 18. Since geology was part of my degree in geophysics, the fieldwork we did opened the door for me to start exploring even though it was initially only around Scotland. I found my geologist colleagues to be avid outdoors people, very social, and very interesting, somewhat creative thinkers, as geology is more like an art than a science. In fact it's like detective work. We'd collect samples, map the area, and make observations and deductions about why certain rocks were where they were.

I graduated in 1991 at age 22 with a degree in geophysics and at that time the options were a career in academia or the oil industry. Given that there were no job opportunities for me then, I stayed in academia, going on to do a D.Phil (Ph.D.). I chose Oxford for many reasons, in particular, the fieldwork in the Alboran Sea near Gibraltar in the Mediterranean especially interested me. This included a couple of six-week scientific cruises where I was required to gather, process and interpret data and link it to other studies and then come up with a reason as to why there was a basin in the Alboran Sea and how it had formed. It took five years to finish my Ph.D. and during those years, I was spending time with colleagues who had enormous vision and who were such go-getters. All that rubbed off on me to the extent that everything felt possible.

While still at Oxford, I applied for and got a job with Shell International, which meant relocating to The Hague. After the three-month basic training course, I was able to talk myself into a job with a small exploration outfit, Shell Prospecting and Development Peru, interpreting data and helping plan surveys in the Amazon jungle. The job was based in the Netherlands. Unfortunately, I never actually went to Peru! But at 27, I was living outside of Britain and loving it.

I was based in the Netherlands until 1999 when an opportunity to go to Dubai presented itself. After the war with Iraq, Iran was starting to open up again, offering foreign companies projects to redevelop existing oil fields. Shell put together a bid to redevelop two oil fields in the Persian Gulf that had been bombed during the war. The initial work was all on paper while I was still based in The Hague. It involved gathering data from around these oil fields, the size of which were uncertain. We knew there was oil there, and we knew, or at least had to consider, that there were probably unexploded bombs on the seabed. I was involved in the logistics of how to gather the data and how to write and evaluate multi-million pound tenders. Once we submitted, and the Iranians agreed, the venture went ahead, a team was mobilized, and I was in.

The logistics of working in Tehran were too difficult, so we set up in Dubai and this is where all the technical work was done. In 2000, on the eve of our departure, my partner and

I married. In the Middle East in order to live together we needed to be husband and wife!

The Hague had never really felt like "living abroad" to me, but the Middle East most definitely did. It was in Dubai that I had my first taste of living in an ex-pat community where it was not unusual for people to talk about this being their "fifth" assigned country, and during a time when there were no emails or regular phone calls home. I learned so much socializing and working with these folk, and work in the oil industry was incredibly well paid. I was 30 and it was a time in my life when I felt like the world was my oyster.

My husband and I love the outdoors so we bought a four-wheel drive in Dubai. We'd head north into the mountains of the UAE and camp out or we'd drive into the desert. In Dubai, my senses always felt stimulated with the mosques staggering the call to prayer, creating an echoing cacophony of sound, and the warm, humid climate amplifying the different smells. The way Emirati women dress in their black *abyas*, some veiled, some not, and the men in their white flowing robes and a *shemagh* wound around their head – it was all so different!

In our home we had a maid, as did all the ex-pats, and I'd always catch a taxi to work and find that the drivers would want to know if I was married. When I said yes, they'd ask if I had children. We didn't at that time. They'd want to know why not – given that the role of women in the Middle East is to have children and run the home.

During our time in Dubai there was an enormous amount of building and development going on, the city was exploding.

Everything was so new, shiny and glitzy. We called it *Fantasyland*. This spilled over into our lives as Shell Dubai threw huge parties for each of its departments every three months – extravagant themed parties. We worked hard, but we played hard too.

After two years there was restructuring within the company. We loved the Middle East and we wanted to stay. I'd heard about jobs in Oman. I took a two-year position with Petroleum Development Oman, transferring to Muscat, where I worked on a joint venture with the Omani government. When I started at this new job, 80 percent of the workforce was Omani and 20 percent was ex-pat. By the time I left 90 percent were Omani and only 10 percent ex-pats. This meant I was working mostly with Omanis whereas in Dubai, I'd worked mostly with British and Dutch, but not Emirati or Iranians.

I gave monthly presentations to the Omani government, quickly learning what information to present and how to present it. This prepared me to mentor up-and-coming Omanis with whom I worked. As a woman, I'd been in the minority at university, and then entered a workforce where about 30-40 percent were women. In Oman the disparity was similar, but older women were absent. Some of the younger women I worked with had had extensive educations abroad, financed by the Omani government, and they were more westernized. Nevertheless, the prevailing attitude was you're either a career woman without children or you marry, have children, and you don't work outside the home.

My work was really rewarding, our social life very active, and our lifestyle super fun. We lived "on camp," which is like a big housing estate full of Shell employees, where we were lucky to be part of a crowd around our age with whom we'd also socialize. We'd also go camping together and to the coast, in particular, Turtle Beach, a point where the Gulf of Oman intersects with the Arabian Sea, to see the turtles hatch. From sea level up 2,000 meters to the Sayq Plateau in the high mountains, and then down south to the Wahiba Sands, named after the Bani Wahiba Bedouin tribe, we had so much freedom to explore.

My husband and I also joined the historical society, with both Omanis and expat members. Once, at my urging a group of us got together and camped in the "Empty Quarter" the largest contiguous sand desert between Oman and Saudi Arabia. I'd read about this area in *Arabian Sands*, by British explorer, Wilfred Thesiger. The book recounts the years between 1945 and 1950 during which he traveled and lived in the Empty Quarter documenting the vanishing way of life of the Bedu, the Bedouins of this region.

The downside of our time in Oman was that my husband was traveling a lot. His work took him all around the Middle East and consequently he missed many of the wonderful experiences on offer. After two years in Oman, we made the decision to move to Calgary. Canada was an easy country for us. We understood the culture. Nevertheless, coming from Oman where there was say, minimal choice at the supermarket, Calgary astounded us with its abundance. Obviously the climate was vastly different yet we embraced the winters. We were on the doorstop of the Rocky Mountains and we loved backpacking in the summer and skiing in winter. The beauty of the mountains is breathtaking.

In 2006, we both took a month's leave of absence from our jobs and went back to the Middle East. The majesty of the desert, the shifting sands, the changing shape of the dunes, the extraordinary colors – the landscape is magical, stark but stunning and, for a couple of geologists, truly spectacular.

In Muscat we took off in a four-wheel drive and marveled at how much "black top" there was. Many of the roads had been paved during our two-year absence. We flew to Damascus, visiting the Umayyad Mosque with its courtyard reliefs made of gold and exquisite mosaics. It is one of the largest and oldest mosques in the world, and considered by Muslims to be the fourth holiest place in Islam. In the recent war the Mosque was destroyed.

We saw the well-preserved ancient Semitic city of Palmyra where artifacts lay about in the sand. Tragically, this area turned into a battlefield, with ISIS blowing it up for the sake of news coverage.

In Aleppo, we found ourselves to be the only foreigners and the main point of interest for the locals, who were out in the streets celebrating a Muslim holiday. We visited the gently lit covered souks, the mosques and madrassa, shops where storeowners spoke several languages and were obviously highly educated and erudite. It's hard to comprehend that what we saw has gone, places of beauty bombed into obliteration, and the people we met and talked with probably dead.

Back in Calgary, I continued to work for Shell, and after a year, our son was born. We'd put down roots, found a great community, the outdoor lifestyle suited us, and we liked the ethos of Canada, the humility of the people and the safe neighborhoods. It felt like a great place to raise our son, so we successfully applied for Canadian citizenship, since Canada is where we will eventually return to live.

My husband continued to travel with his work, not ideal, but then his company folded. Other opportunities appeared and they were mostly abroad, which is how we came to Portugal five years ago. In Canada we were aware of the "cookie-cutter" appearance of everything. There isn't the history and the antiquity so present in Europe, such as the Roman and Moorish ruins in Lisbon. Beauty is absent in the newness of a city like Calgary.

Moving around a lot, as we do, I felt the need for an anchor. For that reason we have a house in Scotland and we go back to our roots at least once a year. Without that, there's the risk of feeling adrift, of not belonging to any particular place. I've seen this in second-generation ex-pats: they know where they were born, where their parents were born, but they don't know where they belong. I didn't want this for our son.

The cycle of making friends, losing friends, starting over every few years in a new country, I find this part of the ex-pat experience emotionally challenging. Despite this, I love the adventures and experiences we've had and continue to have, sometimes it feels like my life is a post-doctorate in cultural anthropology.

And my son, who has been traveling since he was 6 months old, knows the airport routine. He knows how to conduct himself in some very different situations. At 10, he has friends who've already lived in several different countries.

In contrast, I grew up with people who lived on the same street all their lives.

Where is she now?

Audrey, her husband and son, moved this summer to a neighborhood outside of Cascais, to a slightly bigger house with a yard. They hope to add a puppy to the family in the next few months. She tells me that they'll be in Portugal for at least another five years and she confirmed that their plan is to then return to Canada.

Linda Patient

Introducing Linda

For about a year I participated in a weekly improvisational theater group in Estoril near my apartment, which is where I met Linda. Sometimes she drove me home and inevitably we chatted in the car for about 15 minutes before saying our final "goodbye." Her car was often strewn with sports gear, Tupperware and empty juice containers, from the morning swim meet her daughter participated in. It reminded me of how busy her life is juggling 5 a.m. starts, her kids' pre-and-post school programs, and her demanding schedule as a fulltime teacher and department head at one of Lisbon's international schools. The improv theater group, Linda once told me, is her social outing of the week. For sure those Tuesday evenings were fun and it's where I'd see Linda hamming it up, letting her hair down and embracing a couple of hours of total silliness before heading home weary and in need of a good night's sleep in preparation for the next day's early start.

In her words

I'm first generation Canadian though we Canadians don't quite know what it means to be Canadian as we're a mosaic of many nationalities. For a long time I identified with my Welsh heritage. What strikes me when I return to Wales are the similarities: I've always considered myself short and petite and the Welsh are short and petite, and they talk too much and smile too much like I do. I feel I'm with my people.

Both my parents were from the coal mining areas of Tonypandy and Treorchy in the Rhondda Valley, southern Wales. My grandmother encouraged my father to get an education so he wouldn't end up in the mines. Most of his side of the family became professionals and left the Valleys. My father became an architect and then an urban planner. Most of my mother's family still lives in the area, where my grandmother became a local politician. While studying, my father would go back to the Rhondda for the dances, and there he met my mother. Apparently she said to him, "Take me out of this place," and he did. They married and moved to London.

My father worked as an urban planner in London. In the 1950s, there were many exciting career opportunities in Australia, New Zealand, the U.S. and Canada. Dad applied everywhere, received many offers, but for some reason accepted the first offer which was in Edmonton, Alberta. Prairie country. My mom had a baby by this time, my brother Jonathan. She followed my father by boat and they settled in Edmonton, where I was born.

Growing up, my best friend's mother used to tell us we didn't belong in Edmonton, that we were better than a redneck oil and gas town. Her words, and my parents' example, planted the idea that I should leave and do something with my life. In my third year of university, I had an opportunity to go to Montreal. The Canadian government, in attempts to encourage bilingualism and an appreciation and understanding of French culture, offered generous study bursaries. I took advantage, not with the intention of learning French but of spending a summer in Montreal travelling to New York and Boston. The experience was so positive I fell in love with the language and decided I wanted to live in Paris.

It was the mid-'80s and I was a very naïve 23 year old when I started work in Paris as an au pair, which is basically a glorified baby sitter, and as I had a teaching degree, I felt over qualified. The family had a beautiful apartment in the chic Neuilly-Sur-Seine quarter of Paris and my room was in the attic, with only enough space for a bed, cupboard, and desk. I was living in the servants' quarters among other apartments like mine. I became friends with an elderly Spanish maid and at the end of the hall we shared a hole in the floor – our toilet, which we flushed with a bucket! My world had dramatically changed.

In return for carrying out the nanny duties I received free room and board and I had time to go to school and learn French. Six months working, studying and living in Paris caused me to grow up fast and it taught me to appreciate European life, and to understand privilege.

Before returning to Canada, I intended to travel in Europe with friends to celebrate my 24th birthday; since they were taking too long to organize themselves, my parents, who had come to Paris for my birthday, invited me to join them on their tour of France, to be the interpreter, they said. It turned out to be a spontaneous adventure full of laughter, wrong turns, and deep philosophical discussions – one of the happiest and most unforgettable trips with my parents.

The trip did not end as it was supposed to in Normandy's port city of Le Havre. Over our final dinner together, and our sadness at saying goodbye, my mother's eye caught a beautiful wall poster of The Emerald Isle. And just like that, we immediately changed our plans and arranged to be on the next ferry to Ireland, followed by rediscovering my parents' familial roots in Tonypandy, Wales.

At some point I did meet up with my friends and our travels took us to Greece, where I met the man whom I would marry. Dave's father had worked in the oil and gas industry and they'd moved often. He'd gone to 13 different schools growing up while living in Holland, Denmark, England, and Canada. I wanted to leave Alberta and see more of the world, so meeting this international man was propitious.

When my year abroad came to an end, I began teaching in Sherwood Park, Alberta at my old high school, replacing my French teacher. Even though she'd recommended me, I felt like an imposter. I could communicate well in French, yet it was far from perfect, and I'd never trained to teach the language. My plan was to stay only a year, since my dream was to go to Japan and teach English.

Before I moved to Japan, Dave talked me into going to Sydney, Australia with him. He'd found an opportunity to do one term at the university of New South Wales. When my first year of teaching ended, I moved to Vancouver to live with Dave who was working on his MBA at the University of British Columbia (UBC). That summer I studied Japanese and in September, as planned, we went to Sydney and found a great apartment in Bondi Beach. Also, I found a job as a "Kelly Girl," a temporary receptionist placed in interesting companies all around Sydney. My favorite was a tugboat company, where I answered the phone while looking out at Sydney harbor!

By the end of the year I was in Japan. My childhood friend from Canada joined me with the intention of finding a job as a model. Dave came too and the three of us spent a memorable Christmas in Tokyo after which Dave returned to his studies at UBC. A couple of days later, my girlfriend announced she was leaving too. The thought of living and working on my own in Shinjuku, a densely populated and active commercial center in Tokyo, made me really nervous.

Fortunately a student at the school where I worked was looking for teachers to live in his house. He'd quit his job to look after his gravely ill mother and needed to rent out rooms to earn money. He specifically requested Canadians as he'd been to Toronto and liked the people. I was one of three female teachers selected to live in this house, but we soon discovered our landlord was looking for a wife. None of us were interested.

Life in Tokyo was "sensory overload." I loved the excitement but felt overwhelmed by the constant sounds, new smells, and visual stimulus, particularly after working long hours. Dave´s suggestion to leave Japan earlier than I had planned, to start a life together, was a welcome idea. With my pockets full of earnings from my Tokyo teaching gig, I rendezvoused with him for a vacation in the resort town of Puerto Vallarta on Mexico's Pacific coast. The contrast of leaving the metropolis of Tokyo and arriving in the paradise of Puerto Vallarta was stunning.

We settled together in Calgary and I taught French and Humanities with the Calgary School Board. We married when I was 27 and after four years, we explored volunteer opportunities with a Non-Governmental Organization, but couldn't get a placement as a couple. So we sat down with a bottle of wine, opened up an atlas, and decided that if we were going to do this, co-create a life living and working abroad, we needed to make a decision about where. We chose France.

Just after my 30th birthday, we quit our jobs, stored our belongings and left Calgary. We had no idea where in France we'd live or what we'd do for work.

After a short trip to visit family and friends in the U.K., we boarded a bus in London for Bordeaux. We visited many towns in the south, but when we arrived in Montpellier we knew it would be our new home; as a university town it has a certain beauty and energy. Initially we had difficulty finding a home and jobs, but it worked out. And then after two years, I started to think about having a family. I was 32.

The French have an expression, "I feel good in my skin." I did *not* feel good in my skin. I felt homesick for Canada. We decided on Vancouver – another difficult place to find work and a very expensive city, however, again, we were attracted to the beauty of the city and environs and to the lifestyle.

We lived in downtown Vancouver, in the heart of the gay district, the West End, where we'd hang out with our gay neighbors in cafés. Our children, a boy and a girl, were born there, and I was teaching part time. During the Vancouver Olympics there was a crackdown on the drug problem, particularly in China Town and other inner city areas. Our neighborhood was getting a bit edgy too. Drug addicts slept in the parks and playgrounds. It no longer felt like a good neighborhood to raise a family.

We moved close to the university where I was teaching and where Dave was working on his Ph.D. A friend called our new neighborhood "White Rhodesia" because there the homes were worth millions. We were renters and we didn't belong. We did, however, make life-long friends and it was a safe and happy neighborhood for our children.

After 11 years in Vancouver, we decided the kids would benefit from the different life experiences of living abroad. I missed the quality of life in Europe, something as simple as people sitting around the dinner table enjoying meals together. We'd loved France, and so somewhere south and near the Mediterranean appealed. Dave sent out his CV and when the offers came in we had a choice between Lisbon, Dublin or Singapore.

Someone once said to me, "We're either pulled to the past or to the future." Something was obviously pulling me to the past, because when we came to Lisbon for the final interview, what felt right to me was the experience of "Old Europe."

In 2006, when the kids were 9 and 6, we moved to Portugal. At first, I wanted to live in a Portuguese neighborhood, make friends and learn to speak Portuguese, so we moved to upper Parede. Our realtor said, "You won't last long here, you'll want to be in Cascais with all the other foreigners." And to an extent she was right.

Meeting people was difficult. And we had an unfortunate incident involving a neighbor who didn't like where we parked. Instead of leaving a note on the windscreen, they scratched the side of our car with a key. I felt discouraged. Until at a luncheon, sitting at a table with international women, all married to Portuguese, I was given some useful advice: "Don't even try to integrate, we've lived here for years and it's almost impossible. If you really want to make friends, get involved in the expat community." For most Portuguese, the primary relationships are family and old family friends, which take up a significant amount of time. My Portuguese teacher concurred.

I joined IWP and made many friends, and one British friend, a journalist, became my business partner. Combining our skills, we created an English language service-provider company. We taught a business English course at the university, and I also helped students write resumes, and people prepare for job interviews conducted in English, such as a woman who interviewed with L'Oreal in Paris.

And then my business partner's husband, who worked for NATO, was posted to another country. With no interest in running our business on my own, I let it go and started teaching at St. Dominic's International School where the International Baccalaureate program is very similar to the Canadian curriculum. Three years later, Dave was invited to teach at Massachusetts Institute of Technology (MIT). It was an opportunity he could not refuse but he wouldn't go unless we went as a family. We took the kids out of school, I took a leave of absence, and we lived in Boston for six months.

Shortly after returning to Portugal, I started working at Oeiras International School (OIS). My students are approximately 50 percent Portuguese. Many affluent families seem to prefer to send their children to English, French and German schools. Currently, I'm head of the Humanities Department, and I teach English as well.

It's unlikely my children will stay in Portugal but I believe they will always see Portugal as their home. I can't see retiring where we grew up or lived in Canada, even though I miss my family and good friends; the mild Portuguese winters are so livable compared to Canada's 40 below zero temperatures! For now our plan is to launch the kids and then we'll be free to consider if we want to live and work elsewhere or take a sabbatical for a period.

Where is she now?
Linda is still teaching at OIS and living in Parede. Her son is studying and working in Canada and her daughter has finished secondary school and contemplating "where and what next." Linda and her husband Dave are now 12-year fulltime working residents of Portugal.

Isabelle Metairon

Introducing Isabelle
On a foodie's walking tour of Lisbon's Campo de Ourique neighborhood, I overheard Isabelle talking about her childhood in Paris, of sitting under the piano playing house with her dolls while her mother, a concert pianist, practiced. This image was so evocative I wanted to know more. It was a challenge to pin Isabelle down for a longer conversation as she lives a very mobile life, moving between several European cities, and the United States, where she and her husband, an officer with the U.S. Navy, lived off and on. Retired now, her husband is still "ready to go" at the drop of a hat. Preparing to deploy has been the nature of his adult working life, and Isabelle, ever adaptive, is happy to go along as she's used to creating a home and community wherever she is. Although, she hasn't always followed her husband, as she had a career of her own and two children to raise.

In her words
I was born in the 16th arrondissement of Paris, close to the Arc de Triomphe. The apartment was on the fifth floor so my mother walked up and down all the stairs pregnant with me. A midwife came to the house, which was fairly common in 1959. My father was there too, with the family cat. They had just rescued this cat and apparently she was very curious, watching my mother birthing me, and afterward, my father introduced the cat to me.

Later, the cat saved my life. The story goes that I was in my crib struggling to breathe as my baby pillow was blocking my nose or mouth. My parents were busy in the kitchen at the end of a long hallway and had no clue. The cat kept coming to my father and tugging on his pants and then it would run down the hallway to my room and back to my father. After a few laps of the hallway, my father followed the cat to my room, thank goodness!

My mother went back to work three weeks after I was born. She was a pianist and would tour with several different European ballet companies. She was also the rehearsal pianist for Opéra Garnier, and a piano teacher. When she was away, my father looked after me. He was a violinist and saxophonist. Most often musicians have concerts in the evening and on the weekends, so my mother would hire students to watch me – in France they are called governesses, though the girls through my childhood were not formal governesses. I also went to a childcare facility when I was 2 or 3, and sometimes when my father was unavailable, and my mother couldn't find someone to watch me, I went to work with her where I would end up under the piano while she played.

At home, under the piano near my mother also became a place where I would naturally set up house with my dolls. It was a great place to be for a small child as I was out of the way, it was familiar and I was close to my mother and close to the music. Music became a positive conditioning tool for me. Later when I was studying, my father would be in the bedroom practicing the violin, and my mother in the living room on the piano, and I would be in my bedroom studying. Eventually I realized I studied best with classical music in the background.

Needing a more stable work contract and income for our family my father auditioned for the Symphony Orchestra, for Strasbourg radio and television. He got the job and we moved to Strasbourg when I was about 4. I would go with my mother to hear my father perform with the symphony and there I learned audience etiquette as the concerts were recorded live for radio and television. My mother got a position at the Strasbourg conservatorium and ended up teaching there with great success for many years. My father's mother came to stay with us for part of the year and during that time, she taught me how to read, and she taught me English.

My grandmother was born in 1881. On her long walk into the nearby village to go to school there was a distant neighbor who spoke English. She learned English from this person and she became so proficient that during WWII she worked at the U.S. military headquarters in France as a translator. In those days some of the wives came over from the U.S. to be with their husbands. My grandmother kept in touch with one of the American wives who she'd made friends with and when she was old and couldn't see well, I would write her letters to this woman in California.

In France, at the start of the school year, each pupil fills out a card with name, age, siblings and parents' profession. Both my parents were in "the arts" and this was considered problematic as my teachers instantly judged that I would not do well academically, coming from a home where both parents were musicians. This prejudice followed me through high school. Still, I had a very assertive advocate in my mother who defended me, reminding my teachers that their attitude was unfounded. It was because of my mother's support that I was able to focus on sciences.

My father struggled with the attitudes of the school. He was a French soldier during WWII and was captured by the Germans and held as a prisoner-of-war. The trauma left him less spirited than my mother. Also, my mother was a teacher and understood that "there are no bad students, just bad teachers," this was her belief and she stood by it! However, when I sat for my Baccalaureate, I failed, a shock to me, and my parents. As my mother had confronted teachers about their discriminatory attitudes, she thought that my "fail" was in fact both vindictive and political.

During the two years prior to sitting my Baccalaureate, my parents worked hard to organize for me to live with my grandmother's American friend so I could study in California. My father was very conservative and really strict, for instance, he did not like me going out, not even to say, a movie with a friend, but he totally supported the idea of me getting on a plane at 17, even though I'd never flown before, and traveling to America to live with a woman he'd never met!

The Americans had liberated him from Trier, the German camp where he was held as a prisoner-of-war, and where he had been involved in intelligence. After the liberation, learning of my father's part in an underground movement against the Nazis, the Americans wanted him to work with them, but he said no, that he was too ill. I believe at some level he always regretted that decision as the U.S. for him was a bit like the "holy land." Later in his career as a musician, he got to tour the east coast of the U.S. playing 20 or so concerts and he had a great time and so when it looked like I might have a chance to study there, he absolutely wanted me to go.

When I arrived in the U.S., my spoken English was not so good, but I could read and write. I listened and watched a lot of TV and this helped my confidence when I finally started to speak in English. My parents had enrolled me in a Catholic High School as a senior. I audited the classes and at the end of the year, for the second time, I took the Baccalaureate exams, but this time at Le Lycée Français in Los Angeles. When I passed, this confirmed my parents' suspicion that the "fail" from my French school had been political.

With a European Baccalaureate, I was accepted into a Biology program, graduating several years later from University of California Santa Cruz, with a Bachelor's in Marine Biology. My focus was the effect of pollutants on the development of sea urchin larvae. Historically, sea urchins have been used in labs as they breed profusely and thus there's an abundant supply of larvae, and also, due to their sensitivity to contaminants, larvae are great indicators of ocean pollutants.

I went back to France to continue my research and while there, enrolled in a preparatory program for Ph.D. students. At the end of that program, I defended a thesis based on the results of my research. During my undergraduate studies, my research had involved raising sea urchin larvae in the lab, a highly specialized skill that not many people knew how to do. The professor who'd taught me had gone to Puerto Rico. He contacted me as he was looking for graduate students to work with him. I was very interested in what he was doing and so I decided to pursue a doctorate program in Marine Sciences at the University of Puerto Rico. I applied and got a scholarship.

While doing my Ph.D., I met Oscar, whose family is from El Salvador in Central America, although, he grew up in

California. He was a graduate student doing research for his Master's. Toward the end of my program, I took a six-month sabbatical from my thesis work and traveled to northern California to give birth to our daughter in Oakland.

It took me five years to earn my Ph.D., and the results of my research were counterintuitive to the prevailing understanding of sea urchins' larval development: in the absence of nutrition, the larvae increased the length of their feeding apparatus (larval arms) to gather more food. When the food is abundant, the reverse is true. This led me to develop an equally passionate interest in human nutrition.

I applied for post-doctoral work and ultimately pursued a project on Lee Stocking Island in the Bahamas with a private marine science lab to study the larval phase of the Queen conch lifecycle. The findings were for use in fisheries management. I submitted my proposal, it was accepted, and I went with our daughter. Oscar had been accepted into the U.S. Navy's Officers' Candidate School in Newport, Rhode Island.

My position lasted a year. It was really challenging, as I was single parenting our baby while doing my lab research. I ended up with fibromyalgia that included body pains, fatigue, and muscle weakness. In order to recuperate, I went to Rhode Island to be with Oscar. While there we married, but my health was still poor. Oscar headed off on a Navy ship to Florida and I went to Florida too, and stayed when he was then sent to Virginia Beach to do more training. So I could get well, my husband took our daughter with him. She went into daycare and after work he had the opportunity to learn what it's like to single parent!

We based ourselves in Jacksonville with my husband coming and going on various deployments. My health improved, my daughter went into Montessori school, and I found a part-time job with a broker for various health food companies. Three years later, we moved to Rota on the Bay of Cadiz in Spain for Oscar's next duty station. Our son was born two months before we moved.

While in Rota, I enrolled at a school in Seville to study Naturopathy, with a specialization in classical homeopathy. I studied in Spanish, which I'd learned in school in France and I'd also used it while in Puerto Rico. At 35, I was the oldest student at the school. I started practicing as a traditional naturopath in Spain, but that was short lived as we moved to Monterey, California for my husband's next duty station.

Moving, changing schools, a new language, it was hard for the kids. And then two years later, Oscar got a job in Stuttgart, Germany. We decided the kids and I would live in Strasbourg where I had grown up and where my family still lived.

The move was hardest for my daughter. At 13 she'd made good friends in California and was really beginning to find her way as a teenager. When we moved to Strasbourg France, she was not well received by the French teens. We were there four years. During the second two years, my husband was deployed on an aircraft carrier out of Jacksonville, Florida. He was going to be at sea for most of those two years. I opted to stay in France with the kids so they could stay in the same school for a total of four years without another move to another culture and another language. It worked out well as my mother was ill and needed me, and so too did the kids.

When the four years were up, we moved back to Florida and my daughter entered her senior year of high school.

After moving in August to the Mayport Navy base in Florida, I joined a collaborative wellness practice with other natural health practitioners, consulting on a pro-bono basis and offering workshops on nutrition and natural health. Just as my work was really taking off, I got a call from my husband. It was October, he said, "My next duty is in Chile starting in December". That was too soon to uproot the kids again, so Oscar went ahead, and the kids finished their school year in Florida and then we moved to Chile to join him.

Our daughter graduated from high school and successfully applied to university in Chile. Our son wanted to go back to school in Strasbourg, France so I organized for him to stay with a host family, where he lived for a year.

My husband's job in Chile was only for two years, after which he was sent to Miami. While he was in Miami, I was in Jacksonville and my son came back from France to live with me and go to school. Luckily, I was able to join the same group of natural health practitioners I had started with a few years back. My son graduated secondary school and we moved back to Chile where Oscar had been stationed for a second tour of duty. Meanwhile, our daughter had moved to Los Angeles from Argentina where she had been studying.

After that second posting to Chile, my husband was offered a job with the U.S. Embassy in Portugal. We lived from 2013 till August 2016 in Chiado, the neighborhood right in the center of Lisbon. And then Oscar retired. Though that did not slow him or us down.

These days, we move between several European cities where we spend months or perhaps just weeks. We come and go from Spain where we have an apartment that is rented and where all our household effects are in storage. I also attend a biannual classical homeopathy seminar in Belgium. When in Lisbon, Oscar has a part-time job, which he loves, transporting tourists around the city in a Tuk-Tuk.

We also go out to California to see my husband's family and our daughter who is still based in Los Angeles. Our son recently finished his graduate degree at the University of Malta, and we visited frequently while he was studying.

I would like to have just one place that we call home and we're planning on trying to create something like that, but we've been on the move all our married life and I can't imagine settling in one place long term. I've learned how to be very adaptable and wherever I am, I choose to be there completely. I immerse myself and I'm very present to my life in that place for whatever amount of time I'm there.

Where is she now?
It's the summer of 2018, and Isabelle and her husband are in Virginia in the U.S. where they're renting a farmhouse while volunteering at a bee sanctuary. Isabelle will be back in Lisbon in the fall en route to the seminar she attends in Belgium twice a year. And for sure, once here, she'll pick up with her Lisbon life and friends as though she never left.

Sally Hastings

Introducing Sally

No matter where you are, sometimes the world feels small and intimate as though very little separates us from one another. I was reminded of this after meeting Sally a year into living in Portugal. I discovered that her sister and brother-in-law live two blocks from where I lived for many years in Boulder Colorado, patronizing the same neighborhood coffee shops, cafes, and market. Sally said she and her husband had visited Boulder on a number of occasions, as they were contemplating moving there. I never met Sally's sister or Sally until I came to Portugal. I find situations such as this very curious: when people pass one another like ships in the night until circumstances prevail in order that they finally meet. It leaves me feeling that there is some sort of divine order in the universe, especially after I learned of Sally's fairytale story of 'being in the right place at the right time' which led to a 35-year career in the entertainment industry.

In her words

My parents belong to an unusual religious group, considered to be a sect by some. Their belief system shaped my childhood, and the Midwest of the United States, which is where I grew up. Although raised in the suburbs, my parents owned land in undeveloped countryside where we'd visit on weekends. It was rustic: we used an outhouse! We had horses, mostly for decoration, but I rode them sometimes. Our neighbor had cattle and I would ride with him to round them up.

My parents' religion takes the bible literally believing that Jesus never used medicine to heal anyone, since God says we're perfect as we are. In my childhood home we didn't use any medicines and we didn't go to doctors or hospitals. I'd take a note to school excusing me from receiving vaccines or any kind of medical treatment. Fortunately I never broke a bone; if I had, the solution would've been to tape a plank of wood to the limb and pray. It's a religion for the courageous.

One of my childhood friends remembers me telling her, "Don't worry, one day you'll be one of us too." I had been taught that it was the best and only religion and that someday everyone would *see the light* and convert! However, it has worked for my parents, who are in their '90s. They've never been to a doctor, and they've never taken an aspirin. I broke away in my early teens, but it still took me a long time to be able to say, "I don't believe" without fearing that lightning would strike me down. I'm now leery of all organized religion.

At 15, I lied about my age to get a job at the local movie theater selling popcorn and movie tickets. All my 16-year-old friends were working part-time after school and I wanted to too. Six months into my job, an agent from a famous modeling agency in Paris came to my city. She dropped into a photography studio, where she saw pictures of me, which were hanging up to dry. She got my details and drove immediately to the movie theater to meet me. We then went to my home and she asked my parents if they'd agree to let me go with her to France to model. Two weeks later, the time it took to get a passport, I was on a plane to Paris. I'd just turned 16.

I was a very naïve girl. I didn't know what I was getting into. I didn't even know where France was on the world map. It was actually my parents who thought the opportunity to model in Paris was great and that I should go. Later I asked them, "What were you thinking!" My mom said, "Well we just knew that you would always do the right thing." They were incredibly naïve too.

Arriving in Paris the culture shock was like, "Wow, these people don't speak the same language as me." I was very straight-laced from my religious upbringing: still a virgin, didn't smoke, didn't drink. The agents I worked for teased me relentlessly saying, "When are you going to lose your virginity?" "I'm sixteen," I said, "Give me a break!" From a quiet conservative life in the Midwest to Parisian nightclubs till 4 a.m. where everybody was drinking and smoking and my agent was doing lines of coke – it was wild!

Fortunately I was lucky, just really lucky as I had lots of work. And I had the right look for the time: the all American girl-next-door made popular by Christie Brinkley who was one of the first super models. I was a less expensive version of her. The work involved continuous travel, to Germany, Italy, Hamburg, Frankfurt, Milan or a trip to where the sun was bright, like the Canary Islands of Northern Africa. This was in the days when sunlight was needed to get the details of the clothing. There was one year when I took 87 flights. I didn't have time to get into drugs, smoking and alcohol, especially since I needed to be fresh the next morning for a shoot or to fly somewhere.

That year I also met my first boyfriend, fell in love, and moved in with him. The relationship grounded me, even though it wasn't the healthiest. He was 33 and I was 16 and there's a reason why 33-year-old men don't date women their own age and that's because women their age wouldn't put up with them. I mean he had a *Lolita* infatuation! But he was a gorgeous male model and he knew the ropes of the industry, and he wasn't a night-clubber as he'd been there, done that.

In retrospect this relationship probably wasn't so bad. It kept me removed from the underbelly of the industry. A 16-year-old Californian girl that I'd lived with for a while had a lot of wrinkles around her eyes from sun damage. In those days, someone was paid to manually retouch pictures and this was very expensive, so this girl got less and less work and ended up drifting into the nightclub scene. I had another roommate who didn't get enough work and eventually she couldn't afford the rent. My agency dropped her and wanted to send her home, but she refused to go. She ended up living in a dormitory owned by friends of wealthy Arabs and the dormitory was more like an escort agency.

It was an exciting time in my life, but I was plagued by anxiety about whether I was good enough, in particular whether my body was perfect enough. I always watched my weight. It was a constant struggle. I'd go into the agency once a week and get weighed. Although I knew I wasn't perfect, I had a sense of professionalism that really worked in my favor. I knew every position to make the clothes, even the ugliest polyester hausfrau-dress, look great.

After four years in France, traveling all over Europe, I wanted to give New York a try. I was 20 by this time and the agency

I was with in Paris, was working with Eileen Ford, the big American modeling agency. Ford ended up not taking me. I wasn't quite tall enough and I didn't have the newly in-fashion exotic look. I went with another agency that did want someone with my look. This was good for me as Zoli, the agency, had a commercial division and I had the opportunity to do commercials. I was with them for about four years before going to another agency where I did lots of catalogue work in Connecticut, Boston, Philadelphia – lower markets, but I was still making a living.

When I was still with Zoli, I did photo tests for two different products for a famous cosmetic brand. At this point I'd been working for years, nevertheless I was nervous during the shoot as it was a *huge* opportunity and I'd never done anything that big.

It was a straightforward process: my images were compared with the images of several other models and the chosen model would be the face of the campaign. When they contacted my agency, they said they weren't happy with me; saying I was "too stiff in front of the camera." Later, I was in California and I saw products on the shelves using my image! I took samples back to my agency and fortunately I ended up getting paid big money. Sometime after, I visited my dear commercial agent in the hospital just before he died of a mysterious illness. This was the early '80s and AIDS was just starting to take a toll.

The reason I was in California was unrelated to the test shoot. I was to appear on a TV show called Star Search. They had a modeling and acting category and I'd been chosen to compete on the show in the acting category.

I had no real interest in acting so not surprisingly I lost to a former playboy bunny. However, my partner in the acting scene won.

My career peaked in my early 20s. Getting older you make less and less money. The crazy thing about modeling was that I made more money between the ages of 16 and 22 than I've made since. Sometimes I think if I'd been sportier, if I'd kept in shape, had taken better care of my body, maybe my modeling days would've lasted longer.

I ended up going to Bartending School in New York, where I became a "certified mixologist." I needed to train to do something else, and that spurred me on to get my GED, the high school equivalency diploma. I had missed the last two years of high school as a result of leaving for Paris at 16. I also went to trade school to get a Tour Management Diploma and a license in Radio Operating, in case there were opportunities in radio. Ironically the bar tending was the only thing I actually used, and that was back in Europe.

By the time I was 27, I'd been in New York six years and I started to really tire of it. I had a boyfriend and I was hoping it would progress, but it didn't. I missed Europe, so I sent my portfolio to some agencies in Spain. I spent about a month in Madrid, earning enough to live on and travel. In Barcelona I met a girl who was with an agency in Zurich. I sent them my portfolio. I contacted another agency in Geneva, where I ended up moving, living in an apartment with two other girls who worked for the U.N. From there, I went to Athens, where I hit rock bottom. I felt like the tired 'has-been' living in a cheap hotel filled with much younger, bright-eyed models who all had high hopes, but who I knew were not likely to make it in the business. It was all so depressing.

I moved back to Geneva and did a bit more modeling and I answered an ad seeking a proofreader. The former ambassador to Afghanistan wrote for a magazine and English was not his first language. I proofread for him and was his secretary.

Around that time, I met my first husband, a Frenchman. We moved to Lyon, France, where I met a guy who had a group that I sang with in a piano bar. Six months later, we moved back to Neuchatel in Switzerland. There, some local musicians were looking for a singer for their rock band. These kids were maybe 16 to 25 years old and I was about 28. I started singing with them – my husband was older, but I was not quite ready to let go of my twenties. I moved back to Paris after my first husband and I separated.

In Paris, I met a man in show business, who is the man I've been married to for 22 years now. He had put together a touring show for a world famous cabaret. He hired me as a dresser and when the French work permit came through, I divorced my first husband.

I was in my early 30s when I started with the show. I had this sense of sadness as my life was really changing. The days of being center stage, surrounded by the makeup artist, the hairdresser, the photographer, and the stylist were over. Making the transition from model to dresser was a shock. I was on tour with girls 10 years younger than me and suddenly I was really aware of my age.

Lebanon was the first stop on the tour. We were there for the reopening of the Beirut Casino. It was a really big deal, with the press and photographers meeting us on the tarmac. Some of the girls had makeup on and some didn't. Some were pretty and some weren't. Regardless, the photographers wanted pictures of the young dancers. They represented youth. For the first time in my working life, nobody wanted to take my picture. I felt invisible. It was a painful realization but at the same time, I felt incredibly free! I no longer obsessively cared about my appearance, after all nobody was looking at me. I could wear what I wanted, eat what I wanted, and I was still traveling.

I toured with the show for five years. I learned how to repair any costume that needed to be back on stage as well as the maintenance and care of them. Then my husband started his own touring dance show. We toured for another five years. I became the Wardrobe Mistress. I was my own department without supervision.

One tour took us to Florida and we started thinking, "Why are we living in Paris with the really grey winters when we can live in sunny Florida and run the show via the Internet."

My husband was born in Portugal. He was raised in France and had spent 20 years of his professional life touring with the entertainment industry in the U.S. When I met him, we were speaking in French and he could tell from my accent that I was American. He'd spent roughly the same amount of time in the States as I had spent in Europe and during the same years so we mirror each other's history. He had always lived in a country where he wasn't quite French, not quite American, while still feeling European. I felt that way when we went back to live in Florida. I didn't feel American anymore. I'd spent half my life in Europe.

When my husband was offered a contract to do shows at the casinos in Portugal we said yes. We bought a house about a 15-minute drive from one of the casinos and I can't imagine living anywhere else now. I'm putting down roots, literally. We've planted a wonderful garden of fruit trees and flowering shrubs.

Now that I've lived in Portugal for seven years, I'm pursuing citizenship. I've dedicated significant time to learning Portuguese and I want to integrate as much as possible. It took me forever to learn French so it's been challenging for me to learn another language, but I want to sit down at a dinner party and understand everything and these days I do get at least 70 percent of the conversations.

I no longer have a formal job. My husband's latest venture, an urban dance show, does not require wardrobe help. The dancers wear overalls that are machine washable – no sequins, no feathers, no ironing. I miss not having a salary, being needed by the dancers, and I miss the back stage excitement and being on the road, going from town to town, but I also recognize my physical limits. The heavy labor and long hours I did with the dance companies are not something you do into your 50s.

I see myself as someone who has had a career in the entertainment industry. For a while I thought my industry was insignificant. Modeling and fashion is so superficial but that's entertainment, I guess. It really was a lucky fluke the way it all began when that agent came to my hometown and saw the pictures of me. I don't even know why I had those pictures taken. They were portrait photos. My sisters had some taken and not wanting to miss out, I did too. I was just a straight-laced girl plucked out of Kansas! But I had amazing experiences doing what I did, learning on the go at the school of life.

Where is she now?

When last I visited Sally at her home, I admired the impressive growth in her garden. And now with the addition of a dog and a cat, she and her husband are truly settled. That day, she was hosting a fundraising event for *Animais de Rua* and their Trap-Neuter-Return (TNR) program. TNR catches and neuters stray cats and then either adopts them out or returns them to the outdoor location where they were found. The program is designed to reduce feral cat populations and because Sally noticed many feral cats in her village, she quickly got involved, helping with their fundraising.

Diana Lourenco Hill

Introducing Diana

Diana very kindly offered to meet me once a week in a café to help me with my Portuguese conversation. I've had a number of Portuguese language teachers over the past four years and all erred on the side of lots of grammar homework – not my idea of fun! Diana is an American who's lived 30 years in Portugal so she's fluent in the language, and her pronunciation is clear and precise, helpful for a beginner. Plus, she was happy for us to have basic conversation about practical things such as the cakes on display in the café, our drinks, what we were wearing, and to my delight, grammar was not the focus. Diana is actually a Cultural Anthropologist, and upon learning that she'd collaborated on a book about the Portuguese nobility, I was hooked. I wanted to know more.

In her words

My mother's parents were greenhorns: immigrants from Russia with really strong European accents. They had a little corner store in Brooklyn, New York and my grandmother was into "becoming an American." She was a flapper and an actress and very glamorous. The fact that she was Jewish was of no consequence to her, she wasn't religious at all and she didn't transmit her Jewish heritage to my mother. For her that was about the old country and America was about not being any of those things.

The man that my grandmother married made and lost several fortunes. They had lived the high life on Park Avenue, Manhattan with silver and servants. When the stock market crashed, they moved out to California to start over, but my grandfather had turned to alcohol and so my grandmother divorced him. Consequently, my mother had a very unsettled childhood and after her parents divorced, they lived a peripatetic existence.

At some point my mother became interested in religion, and when she met my father, he was about to enter a monastery to become a monk. He lasted six months. Apparently he kept thinking about my mother. Shortly thereafter they married.

My father's family came over on the Mayflower and then "went out west." They were a big family made up of farmers of German and English heritage. My dad's father was absent a lot as he was an engineer on a train. At one point he moved the family to a farm where my dad learned farming. Later, my father was the first in his family to go to college, eventually becoming a physicist. He wanted to save the world by finding a way to create cheap power for developing countries.

My mother and he left California and their social class and moved to Chicago. In 1966, when I was 5, we moved to Europe as a family. My father, who was doing post-doctorate work in Chicago, had received an offer of another post-doctorate at Oxford. We packed our belongings in trunks and sailed on the Queen Elizabeth from New York to the U.K. After a couple of years, we moved to Geneva in French-speaking Switzerland. There was a little Lebanese girl who was my playmate in the apartment complex in which we lived and I learned French playing with her, even though my sisters and I were in an international school where English was the main language.

My father, who had become a high-energy nuclear physicist, was doing research at CERN, the European Organization for Nuclear Research based in Geneva where physicists and engineers are probing the fundamental structure of the universe. At CERN he started working with super computers. I remember going into the computer room with him and seeing thousands of wires going everywhere. My father then got this wild job offer from the Paris offices of El Paso Natural Gas (EPNG). An American company, with interests in owning and controlling oil and gas pipelines, EPNG wanted to do things like use nuclear explosives to loosen natural gas reserves in the Algerian desert! When we moved to Paris in 1969, they'd figured out via computer simulation what would happen if nuclear energy were used for these reasons.

In Paris, my parents had a kind of bohemian lifestyle. I'd often come home from the American school that I attended and find no one there, so I'd take myself to the Louvre and wander around Paris on my own or with a friend. My parents also rented a place out in the countryside and there were French kids in the village that I used to play with. To this day, I can still speak French. Learning with French-speaking kids my accent is good, but my vocabulary and grammar are not that great.

We were in France when my parents divorced and the family split. I was 12. I think the kind of social changes going on, the Vietnam and Watergate years, contributed to the breakdown of their marriage. A marriage needs all kinds of props to survive and theirs had none. My mom moved back to Chicago, taking one of my sisters and me with her. My older sister stayed with my dad in Paris.

Living in Chicago was a real culture shock, especially attending junior high in the Chicago suburbs. I felt as though I had a foot in two cultures. My French identity was strong and the kids in the U.S. wouldn't let me forget it, they'd call me "Frenchy." I dressed differently too and I had different ideas about things, but mostly I hadn't watched television, which meant often I didn't know what my peers were talking about. So I started to watch TV like it was homework. During the summer and Christmas holidays, I'd sometimes go to Paris to stay with my dad whereas the kids I was in school with might go once into the city to see the ballet or to a football game or something. Obviously I felt different.

In 1979, during my last year at high school, an exchange student from France attended my school and we clicked like crazy. Motivated by our friendship, I started to go to France to visit her, even though at this point my father had moved back to the States, to New Mexico. When I was about 16, I was at a party in Paris, talking with a really good friend of my mom's. I told him how much I enjoyed World History and about other things that I found interesting, he said, "Oh, that's anthropology." I was like, "Oh, ok, I guess I'm interested in anthropology."

When I graduated high school I went to Bard College in upstate New York for undergraduate studies in the liberal arts. I did a senior thesis on Bard's nursery school using language as a tool to study the cultural interactions of the kids. And then my boyfriend at the time moved to Houston, and I decided to go with him. I sat in on some classes at Rice University in Houston and they had a really cool anthropology program. I applied and was accepted.

Generally speaking a graduate degree is a stepping-stone to a Ph.D., but I didn't want to be an academic, but I also questioned the practicality of a Master's in Cultural Anthropology. Around this time, my relationship had ended, and I reasoned that if I did a Ph.D., I'd be able to do research, and maybe in Europe, though I didn't want to go back to France. My preference was to do research of a non-exotic nature and to do field work in a very different way while learning another language.

Portugal came to mind.

In the early 1980s, in my field, no one knew anything about Portugal. I started to read and to talk to people, and to learn Portuguese, while doing my Ph.D. At some point I decided that if I was really serious about learning the language, I needed to be "in country." I applied for summer grant money, and came to Lisbon for a couple of months in the winter of 1985. I stayed in Costa de Castelo and found a language school in the Bairro Alto in the center of Lisbon. Those four months were magical. In 1987, I came back and spent another couple of months working on my Portuguese and this time I also traveled north. When once again I returned to Houston, I applied for research money to do a full Portuguese course in Coimbra, thinking, "If I get the funding I'll stay and do research." At the end of 1988, I got the funding.

The language and cultural intensive course in Coimbra was filled with students several years younger than me, kids in their early 20s who were still interested in having a good time. The common language was English and unfortunately the Portuguese university students were hard to access as they were not interested in the foreign students. I was friendly with an Italian girl who had a car and who also loved to travel, so every weekend we would get in her car and drive some place. In February we went south, following the coast down to the Alentejo.

The sea was really wild, churned up and dramatic. The sky was filled with storm clouds and everything was really green due to the winter rain. It was rural and the people were so different from the people up north. I had this strong feeling of wanting to stay there.

I went back up to Coimbra, packed up, and took a bus to Milfontes, a 20 km drive from Cavaleiro where I was headed, a village near the Alentejo coast. On the bus there was a woman also going to Cavaleiro and we chatted. When we got off the bus together, she walked me to a little store and she said to the storeowner, "This woman needs a place to live," and the storeowner said, "Oh, my daughter-in-law has a place." Within 20 minutes of arriving, I had a place to live, I had neighbors, at least 10 people knew I was there to do research, and this was all in Portuguese. It was a special time.

There weren't many tourists in the area back then. There was a big community of Germans living about 80 kms away, it was sort of a hippy commune and they were quite shocking to the Portuguese who didn't understand what they were doing there and why they were living like that.

The Portuguese, even when traveling a short distance into town, always made the effort to dress, to change shoes, put on a scarf, in a way that indicated they were paying attention, giving a nod to the social environment. They found it disrespectful that people would walk around barefoot in leather vests and pants that they hadn't taken off in about a year. In contrast, the German hippies thought they had an affinity with the Portuguese as they too were living this hardscrabble rural life.

Starting my fieldwork in Cavaleiro, a town of about four hundred, my idea was to listen to people tell their stories and note how the 1974 revolution had entered their narrative. I had read some papers on the oral history of Italians and fascism and how people were inveigled. I went to Cavaleiro with the idea of just listening. I couldn't speak Portuguese that well, but I could understand it so I started cataloguing conversations: What were people talking about? What were they not talking about? What were the silences? And in what circumstances were people talking about *these* things as opposed to *those* things?

The villagers tolerated me following them around, just sitting and listening, and interacting a little, and I was aware that I was having fun and that I was getting a very organic picture. During the day, I was very present to the village conversations and in the evenings I'd write. Very quickly I was also involved in the town's social center, which meant I wasn't just a bystander. Every weekend there were dances either in the surrounding towns or in Cavaleiro. We'd get on the back of scooters and go to the dance in whichever town it was being held and Antonio, the man I became involved with, was part of that crowd that came into town and to the dances.

Two years later, in March of 1991, I returned to the U.S. Over the next 10 months, I visited Cavaleiro a couple of times and then in January of 1992, Antonio came out to the States, we got married, and I went on to finish my Ph.D. in Houston.

For my dissertation I sought to understand Cavaleiro through the narratives I'd catalogued, writing chapters on the different things that people talked about. When you live your life in a community like Cavaleiro, where not much happens, the way you talk about things is your cultural capital. Thus the suggestion of innuendo, having knowledge about some illicit behavior, gives the speaker standing. It's not whether the behavior actually happened, it's more important in the community that someone was able to say, "Well, I saw a white car parked there again at five o'clock" and the interlocutor, says, "What white car?" There was another chapter on material goods: people talked about cows; and unmarried women talked about collecting their trousseau.

I'd spent my life wandering around and I was very seduced by this community, Cavaleiro. The idea of having a sense of place, and a family, encouraged me to convince Antonio that we should return – though I wished we'd stayed in Chicago longer, where we were both working and where our first daughter was born in 1994. We hadn't really given ourselves the time to consolidate our little family, consolidate our parenthood, and when we moved back to Cavaleiro, we ended up living with Antonio's parents with a new baby and we'd only been married two years. It was another two years before we were able to build our own home.

Our second daughter was born in 1998, and when she was 9 months old, I was invited by one of my academic advisors and head of the department at Rice University to participate in a project. George E. Marcus's work was on Elites and Dynastic Families in the United States and Tonga. George was invited to speak at an international conference in Portugal, held at the palace of the Marquês de Fronteira, Fernando Mascarenhas. The Marquês, who was also an academic and historian, liked George and invited him to do a project on the Portuguese nobility. George agreed.

I ran into George while out in the U.S. visiting a friend. He told me about the Marquês and his proposal. I was still in contact with anthropologists in Portugal and I knew of the Marquês and some of the people in his circle. I offered to join the project as a kind of cultural interpreter and translator. At first I spent the night at the palace a couple of times, which gave me a chance to get to know the Marquês, then George came with his family. I joined them and we all stayed at the palace for a month. The Marquês took us up north and we met people he was connected to, people whom he thought we should consider in our research.

After we wrote up the research, we presented our findings at our own small conference to which we invited the Portuguese nobles. We gave them a copy of our preliminary work and afterward met to address some of their questions. They wanted to know who they were: Are we a group? Are we an ethnicity? Are we a tribe? Where do we fit? What's the state of Portuguese nobility in this particular time in history? Obviously we told them what we thought from various perspectives, but beyond that there wasn't really any place to go with it, except we began to think about a book concept based on the research.

George and the Marquês had been communicating via email for a long time before we started the fieldwork and I'd read a lot of those emails. I said to George that from a theoretical perspective those emails were a collaborative project. And indeed a book of their correspondence titled, *Ocasião: The Marquis and the Anthropologist, A Collaboration* was subsequently published in 2005. The book also included the report we presented to the nobles and the book's summary was my impressions gathered in my role as the observer, interpreter and cultural anthropologist.

I could have followed up and done more with the research we gathered, but I didn't want to be an absent mother to my children. As it was, my mother-in-law very much wanted to raise them and I had to fight for my right to be their primary parent. Once back in Cavaleiro things started to fall apart, first at the girls' school, and then I started to feel lonely and isolated. Something was missing for me. Consequently my relationship with Antonio suffered. Some of the anthropologist friends I'd made had their kids in an international school just outside of Lisbon and I began to think my girls should go there too. Cavaleiro's one-room schoolhouse had worked well, but there'd been several years of bad teachers and in a child's life that's too long.

In 2003 the girls and I moved from the Altentejo to Cascais to live, commuting back to the Alentejo on the weekends. It was a way to make me happy – to help me manage the cultural and language differences of life in Caveleiro – plus it would give the girls a good education. My oldest was 10 when we made the move, much the same age I was when my parents divorced. I didn't want to repeat history.

Six months into the move, I started working at the girls' school and fairly quickly I was put in charge of the English as an Additional Language program. And that's what I did for the next 12 years. When both my girls finished secondary school, the youngest one just recently, I resigned.

Now I'm planning on returning to the Alentejo to work on renovating our home while contemplating "what next?" I can't quite imagine a way of returning to Caveleiro to live fulltime without finding myself feeling isolated. Nevertheless, I do feel as though I want to put myself back into a Portuguese environment, to take advantage of speaking the language.

Moving from country-to-country as a child, not really attaching to people or places, I'm aware that it suits me to keep a foot in both the Portuguese community and the ex-pat community. That said, I've been here almost 30 years, so, in fact, I have attached. Until recently, I had these fantasies that one day I would return to the U.S. to live, but the reality is I have a home and a family in Portugal. I can envision returning to do some research or service work and if something should happen to my parents, I'll go back for a period. I feel fortunate that my life and my marriage are flexible enough that I can do this.

Where is she now?
Diana did go back to Caveleiro and renovate the family home. And then out of the blue, there was a family health crisis. For much of the past two years she's been based in the U.S., returning to her home and family in the Alentejo when she can.

Birgit Weber

Introducing Birgit
When I lived in the U.S., a friend referred me to Birgit for acupuncture. Her clinic in Colorado was not far from where I lived. At my first appointment, Birgit handed me "new patient" paperwork and then introduced me to her acupuncture center, set up in one large room with some dividing curtains. A highly functional arrangement, it looked like a clinic in say, India or China, though it was unique to other clinics in Colorado. Birgit was a unique practitioner too: caring but pragmatic, skilled but inexpensive, German yet philosophically Eastern with a strong inner voice – a guiding voice that has nudged her to overcome her fears via travel, and to search for meaning and a greater truth.

In her words
A midwife delivered me in her farmhouse in a village in Bavaria. My grandparents lived there, but my parents lived in a town about four hours away close to Frankfurt. My mother had gone to visit her parents to give birth to me with her mother's support. My childhood looked quite normal on the outside, but it was kind of rough. Both my parents were survivors of WWII and both sets of grandparents had lived through WWI. So there was this intergenerational sense of loss, first a loss of security and then a sense of displacement.

My father was in Italy during the war where he was captured and imprisoned. As a prisoner of war he contracted hepatitis, which he seemed to be dealing with in one way or another for the rest of his life. It was a huge burden for his health and wellbeing. I think the stress, probably post-traumatic stress, which my parents experienced, carried over into our home so that my older sister and I grew up with it too. Consequently, I don't have memories from my childhood of wellbeing or abundance or relaxation.

But, as a family, we did travel a lot for vacations. We drove into Italy and Austria and Switzerland, and we used to bicycle into France. We went to Turkey, and I went to England with my mother, and also Sweden and Denmark. We also went to Yugoslavia quite a bit for summer holidays – it is so beautiful there – and I remember as a child feeling very scared crossing the walled-border into East Germany. When I was 16, I hitchhiked to Greece for three weeks with my boyfriend. In the mid-'70s it was the way to travel and thinking back I was lucky that I was always safe hitchhiking as anything could have happened.

When I was 10 we moved to a town close to the border of France and Switzerland. My father had been offered a very good job at the university. He was a lawyer and the job of Chancellor was prestigious and well paid. I went into a Catholic nuns' school. I really hated it. I wanted to learn but not what and how we were being taught. I just barely made it through high school, a splinter of a point less and I would not have graduated.

Years before, when I was maybe 6, my sister and I would walk 30 minutes to-and-from school and even at this young age, I would sometimes walk on my own. On one occasion, I stopped in the park and I had this clear vision of wanting to know "the truth." I knew even then that I would not have a normal life, that I would not marry and have children, and that there was some impulse within me to find something greater than myself.

Later, when I was a teenager, I had a friend who was a classical pianist and he had these little Haiku stories from Japan that captured my imagination; so much so that I began to crave the opportunity to be in a Zen-like monastic environment. I thought such a place did not exist which made me feel quite sad until I found out that such environments do exist, for instance, in India. Around this time, I kept saying to my mother that I wanted to go to India, but my mother was not interested in taking me. I waited until I was 19 and then I took myself.

University did not interest me as I had my heart set on becoming a handweaver through being apprenticed to a master. My grandmother had passed the love of this craft onto me and through her I found a woman who had a handweaving shop and I worked alongside her learning the craft. I worked 40 hours a week and every six weeks I had a one-week block of schooling in a trade school in Hamburg. The first holiday I had from my apprenticeship, I went to Munich to do a Primal Scream workshop, a therapy that was very popular then. I had a lot of inner turmoil that I wanted to work out. I'd actually tried to enroll in this workshop when I was only 15, but you needed to be 18 or older to participate.

I had worked part time in a pizzeria to save the money to pay for the workshop, and during the workshop we did a meditation in the morning and evening. I asked where the music that accompanied the meditation came from and it was from a guru in India. I also found out that there was a retreat center in Hamburg where I could buy a cassette tape of the music. When I returned to my apprenticeship, I found my way to this center, just walking through the streets asking people for directions.

I loved the center so much that I called in sick to my apprenticeship and I stayed there for a week, after which I would visit regularly to do their sitting meditations. This led me to a guru who at the time was very controversial. Despite this, I became one of his devotees; I wanted to go to India to follow him. I let my employer know that I was leaving the weaving shop, but when I told my mother she was very much against it. However, I packed my things and off I went to India. I was 20 years old.

I landed in Bombay (now Mumbai) and took a bus to the town where the guru lived, and from there I took a rickshaw to the Ashram. I lived for six months in a little bamboo hut by the river about a 15-minute bike ride from the Ashram. It was so different from anything I'd experienced. The people at the Ashram were very direct and upfront, which I discovered during the encounter groups I participated in, but at the same time it all felt so alive, despite the fact that I think most of the time I was very scared. In retrospect, I had so much courage and the will to push through my fear.

I did a Vipassana, a ten-day silent-sitting meditation, in a room where it felt as though mosquitoes were eating us alive. At one point I was really ill, and I just lay in my hut until I healed. Nobody brought me food or water. In India life has a different value, if you die you die, but of course I didn't die. It was all very raw living there and I just threw myself into the experience.

After the first few months, I started to work in the Ashram kitchen, the Ashram bookbindery and the boutique where we sold robes. At around the six month point, my guru went to Oregon in the U.S. America to me was a very scary place, unimaginably scary, so rather than follow him to the U.S., I went back to Germany.

My family was not very welcoming, so I moved to Cologne and into a big Ashram that had a restaurant where I worked as a cook for the next seven-and-a-half years. I then returned to India where I lived another eight years. In 1990 my guru died. I stayed on at the Ashram in India for another two years. By this stage, I could not imagine life outside, given that I'd entered a cloistered environment at 20. I did have a driver's license, but I did not have a bank account. I was completely dysfunctional in a world beyond the Ashram. I was reluctant to leave, but I knew I needed to in order to start a new life.

I decided to go to a country where I'd never been before and where I didn't speak the language and where I didn't know anyone. I wanted to see if I could do it, make a life for myself somewhere totally different. I chose Japan.

I arrived in Tokyo and very quickly found work as a Bunny Girl in a Playboy Club in a very upscale area of Tokyo. It was an amazing experience, completely non-sexual. For example, the men didn't even talk to us or touch us. I worked from 4 p.m. till 8 p.m. and the men came for dinner at the restaurant in the club and we'd light their cigarettes and serve their food and drink while walking about in high heels, bunny ears and tails and heavily made up. There was piano playing in the background. Apart from that nothing really happened.

I made a lot of money, which I needed as Japan was very expensive. I rented a room the size of a closet with a ceiling so low you couldn't stand up straight. The Japanese woman who owned the apartment charged a lot for that room, which I shared with another German girl. We had about one-foot of space between our mattresses on the floor. During my free time I'd take myself around Tokyo to temples and various sites, learning about the culture while exploring.

I had no interest in staying long term in Tokyo, so I returned to Europe to find work. I decided on Italy, where I worked in a retreat center as a cook. I was involved with a man I'd met at the Ashram in India. He was an American from Pittsburg, a student of the martial arts. He was planning on returning to the U.S. to study with an Aikido teacher in Montana. I threw caution to the wind and went with him – a huge risk as our relationship was not good and I'd never wanted to go to the U.S. – the gun culture really scared me.

Between us, we had very little money. Nevertheless, we bought a car, driving it through several states to our destination. Despite all the fears I had had about the U.S. I was totally won over when we drove through Montana. I was so in awe of the natural beauty of the Tetons and Yellowstone National Park. I saw wild roaming moose and buffalo and this was extraordinary to me. To this day, I still feel emotional thinking about that area of the United States. It's truly magical.

When we arrived in Montana, I was 34 and married to my American boyfriend, and I'd been issued a green card so I could work. We were in a university town, so work was hard to find as the students made up so much of the part-time workforce. Regardless, I found a job in a bakery where my shift started at 2 a.m. and where I made minimum wage, around $4 an hour. The bakery work was strenuous physical labor; that, and the early morning hours, meant I was not going to do it long term.

After studying hard to take my American driver's license, which I passed with flying colors, I realized I was ready to go back to school to study a vocation. As a result of being treated by an American acupuncturist while in India, I'd developed a fascination for Chinese medicine. His office was part of the Ashram and in my spare time I would go to his office and help out. My interest hadn't waned and this gave me the courage to apply for acupuncture school in Colorado. I was accepted and within a week I moved from Montana to a university town near Denver. My husband came too, though at this point we were separated and just friends.

The three years of study at the acupuncture school was really challenging, made more so by the fact that many of the teachers were Chinese and I had trouble understanding their English, and I also did not have the English vocabulary to grasp everything that was being taught. I was so determined to succeed, I studied from the moment I got up until I went to bed, and this was in between going to school or working at my part-time job cleaning houses.

I was also incredibly lucky as I found an extraordinary mentor very soon after starting school. A couple came to one of my classes as guests. They were both Chinese doctors, and doctors of acupuncture, and he was also a highly respected spinal surgeon. Although the wife spoke no English, I was immediately drawn to her. I wanted to work with her. I found out where they lived and through a series of meetings, we agreed that I would be her apprentice, which meant that for the next three years, I went to her home twice a week to study with her and to be treated by her.

This woman became my primary teacher and advisor on acupuncture and the herbs of Traditional Chinese Medicine. After I graduated I worked with her, observing directly the remarkable results her patients experienced under her care. We stayed in contact over the years and when I eventually went on to set up my own clinic, I always reached out to her when I needed to consult with an expert over a difficult case.

When eventually I took my final exams and passed, I was so proud but I was also exhausted from three demanding years, so I went back to the Ashram in India for six months and after three months of downtime, I started practicing my new vocation outdoors at the Ashram. People would come and sit in chairs – I didn't have an acupuncture table – they'd pay me what they could, and I had the chance to get over my needle phobia by practicing inserting the needles in my patients. I saw the success of working like this instead of sitting one-to-one with a patient in an office. I could see how healing it was for a number of people to be in the same space being treated at the same time. I decided that I wanted to recreate this style of treating people.

Back in Colorado, I was accepted as an assistant teacher at a school of acupuncture. As an employee, classes were free and I took advantage of this; I wanted to build up my credits and get my Master's degree. Two years later, in 1998, I graduated with an MA and then in 2000, my father died.

Sometimes from loss there is a gift of sorts, and mine was an inheritance that enabled me to buy a home with a yard and a garden.

Now that I was feeling settled and secure, and with a growing acupuncture practice, I started to look for a space that would allow me to recreate the communal experience I'd had treating people at the Ashram. My contemporaries thought I was crazy, but they didn't understand the communal clinic concept. Fortunately, my business partner did and together we opened an acupuncture center with one large room where very comfortable reclining chairs were spread around, and we had one private room for patients who were really struggling and needed privacy. My partner and I would tend all the patients, sometimes up to eight at a time, and it really worked, it was communal healing! Eventually, I set up my own clinic. It was a smaller operation, with two tables divided by a curtain in one room, and two rooms with a table and a reclining chair in each, so sometimes I was seeing maybe five people at a time thereby maintaining this vision of communal healing.

Every other year I would go to Germany for Christmas to see my mother, my sister and her family, and my mother would come to visit me in Colorado during the summer and stay maybe three or four months. As my mother aged, I was aware that I needed to think about whether I should be geographically closer to her in case she needed help. Several years ago, mother really started to decline and I made a couple of emergency trips to be with her. Around that time I thought about moving back to Germany, but I did not want to do that, but I did think about moving back to Europe, I just wasn't sure where.

I practiced acupuncture in Colorado for 18 years before I moved to Portugal. In 2016 everything changed suddenly. In April that year I saw several YouTube videos of a guru that I was familiar with and his message spoke to me in such a way that I knew I wanted go to his center in the south of Portugal. Within weeks I'd found someone to buy my practice and rent my house. Within months, I'd packed up and I was ready to move. It was all very fast and the situation felt similar to when I first went to India. I was freefalling into the unknown.

I'd never been to Portugal and I really had no idea what I was coming to, I was just so drawn to this guru. The timing was right though, as everything came together easily. Plus, Portugal was so much closer to my mother in Germany.

The retreat is outside a small village in the hilly region of southern Portugal. This is where I now live and where I cook in the Ashram kitchen. I love cooking. I always have, even as a small child I loved to cook. Probably vegetarian cooking is the most enjoyable for me. We don't grow the food here. The mountain terrain is too inhospitable for us to grow vegetables. Instead, our produce is delivered from local vendors who farm in the area.

My mother passed away in September 2017 and I'm glad I was closer as I had a number of trips to be with her. I'm not sure where I will be in the future, I still have my house in the U.S., but I'm happy to stay indefinitely at the Ashram, I know I'm welcome here.

Where is she now?
Birgit is still in southern Portugal, cooking at the Ashram she moved to in 2016.

Sandhya Acevinkumar

Introducing Sandhya

Sandhya is a fabulous cook of traditional north Indian food. I know this, as I took a cooking class that she co-taught with an Indian friend. I was excited about participating. I believe you learn the best tips and tricks from practiced home cooks, and that belief was upheld in Sandhya's class. Another time, Sandhya helped facilitate an IWP tour of her community's Hindu Temple in Lisbon where she graciously and intelligently answered naïve questions about her faith from the group of international women. And on still another occasion, we walked alongside one another on a hot summer's-day hike and I found out that she has been in an arranged marriage since her early 20s. I was curious about the cultural practice of arranged marriages and so with great interest and respect, I sat down with Sandyha to learn more about her and the Portuguese-Indian community in Lisbon.

In her words

During the time of the British Raj, my 17-year-old grandfather left Gujarat, India, an area bordering Rajasthan to the north and Pakistan to the west, looking for opportunities. It was the 1890s and he sailed on a Portuguese caravel, disembarking in the Portuguese colony now known as Mozambique. He had very little money and he did not know the language. We know this story well. In our culture the accomplishments of our ancestors are told to the children and the children's children, and it is also written down.

My family is Hindu Brahmin from the region of Gujarat where the people are known as the entrepreneurs of India. My grandfather's courage in leaving his homeland was the best thing because when I go back to India, which is often, I see how relatives and friends are struggling. Life is not easy there, whereas my grandfather grew to be a very successful businessman in Mozambique.

When my grandfather passed away, my father was still quite young. Now a widower, my grandmother took her two sons back to India where she felt it would be safer. By the time my father was in his early 20s, he was in an arranged marriage with my mother, who within a year was pregnant. Leaving my mother and his firstborn, my father went back to Mozambique with his brother to build up a business. He stayed for seven years and during that time, he did not return to my mother and brother. Once he'd achieved the success he sought, he came back to India, collected my mother and returned to Mozambique. My brother stayed in India and went to boarding school and I was born in Lourenço Marques, Mozambique in 1968. My father was doing well by then, his retail business was growing, he had a warehouse and a house and he was also able to send money back to India so that his widowed mother lived well.

My early childhood was charmed.

We lived in a neighborhood of Gujarati immigrants where I grew up with other Indian children. Very early on my father wanted me to learn English so he would bring English-language children's books home and teach me English in the evenings, though Gujarati was our first language. I also learned Portuguese at the *Infantário* or preschool.

My parents were always a bit fearful. There were tensions between the Africans and the colonialists, due to the ongoing war for independence. In 1974, when independence was declared, my parents' fears worsened. The workers at my father's shops were rebelling, and when the name of our city, Lourenço Marques was changed to Maputo in 1976, my father felt it was time to leave. He wanted to get out before it became too chaotic. Also, we knew of two other Indian families that had suffered fatalities when looters had tried to steal from one of their shops.

Leaving Mozambique, we were required to surrender our passports. The new independent government required us to give up our nationality. Consequently, we traveled to India on our Portuguese passports and with only small bags. My mother managed to pack some of her jewelry, but my father lost everything: his properties, his businesses, and his factory. My parents were devastated.

When we reached India I remember that my father was sad for months. Fortunately, my grandfather had left the family real estate. Once my father was ready to start over, he began by renovating one of these properties into a hostel. When it was operating as a business, he suspected that his hostel was being used for prostitution so he closed it down, and of course he lost money, but he was a man of enormous integrity.

Being a Brahmin comes with a lot of responsibility: our behavior and our conduct is held to a high standard, for example, you wouldn't see a Brahmin smoking, drinking or eating meat. And people expect us to know more of the scriptures because centuries ago Brahmins were the priests.

After the hostel, my father started a soap factory in our town, Jamnagar, but he lost money in this business too, so he went back to developing one of my grandfather's properties, this time into a hotel. But I think he felt discouraged. Having grown up in Africa, he was not familiar with ways of doing business in India. Around this time he realized our Portuguese passports were about to expire.

While in Jamnagar, I went to an English Catholic school, St. Anne's, which was run by nuns. I'd returned to Jamnagar from Africa, so the other girls considered me unique and this made me popular. My parents were respected in the community and considered quite sophisticated – my mother decorated the house in a European style, which she'd learned in Portuguese Mozambique.

In 1978, my father came to Portugal to renew his passport and once again in search of opportunities. He stayed for three months, taking out a lease on a shop in Martim Moniz in Lisbon, before coming back to collect us. We moved to Portugal in July 1979, but before we came, my father arranged my 21-year-old brother's marriage. He was fearful he might not be able to find a Brahmin wife for my brother in Portugal. My parents, my brother and his new wife, my grandmother and I, plus, two guests of my father's, traveled to Lisbon where we all moved into a small apartment in Martim Moniz.

We'd had a very comfortable life and lifestyle up until this point, living in spacious homes with home help, and now we were eight people living in a tiny apartment. We all worked in the shop, me too, after I got home from school.

I was only 10 years old and I hated our new life.

When winter came, we were not used to the cold and we did not have proper clothes for the climate. Our Portuguese neighbors would say, *coitadinhos*, poor little things. My mother and sister-in-law wore their saris and the Portuguese would laugh at them. When we went out, we went out together as a large family group and the Portuguese would mock us. It was sad.

I started to feel ashamed of my culture where once I'd felt so proud. Even the color of my skin started to bother me. And this is when I realized I was different to everyone here.

There was only a small Indian community in Lisbon at that time and my father was one of the first Indian immigrants to open a shop. We didn't have a community meeting place then either, so we Indians would gather together in someone's garage and we'd celebrate Diwali, our New Year, in the hall of a Bombeiros – we did this for five years. Over time, I started to make Gujarati friends and our community grew stronger. At the same time, there was real fear of the Portuguese. We could go to their homes, but we could not eat their food as we were vegetarian, and we had always to be careful not to give too much information away in fear that the Portuguese might expel us and send us back to India.

My father put me in an American school, which then was in Carnaxide outside the city center of Lisbon. I was seen as different. My mother put coconut oil in my hair and braided it. That's how we'd do our hair for school in India. She'd also dress me. At 11, we didn't choose our clothes, our parents did. All of this was fine with me but at the American School, I was teased terribly; I had a strong Indian accent and my English grammar was not so good; the school had a strong sports focus and I was not a good athlete – I couldn't even swim!

Each day I caught public transport to school, but most of the students caught a school bus, or they were driven to school by their parents or the family's driver. After-school activities were inaccessible to me. By the time I got home around 5 p.m. I would have a snack and go straight to the shop to work until 7 p.m. After the shop closed, we'd go home and have dinner and only then could I do my homework. My family just worked.

My father wanted to save money so he could buy property. We had plenty to eat, but there were no extras, no luxuries. We had one pair of winter shoes and one pair of summer shoes. During the eight years that I studied at the American school, Dad was working so much he only came to my school twice: on the first day to drop me off, and on the day I graduated. I felt very alone.

When I turned 13, my menses began, but my mother had never told me about menstruation. I was in PE class. I stained my clothes and I was mocked. I went home crying and in quite a state as I had no idea what was happening to my body. That is when my vitiligo started and spread.

Many years later, by the time I was 30, I realized it was the hormonal changes, the shock of starting my period, and the emotional trauma of my early teen years that contributed to the condition. By Grade 7, I had more white patches of depigmentation on my face and my body and I was mocked even more. It was not just the kids at school that mocked me; my parents were cruel too. They would tell me that it was a disease, that I must have done something bad and brought it upon myself, and as a result, no one would marry me and I'd end up alone.

I started to distance myself from my family, especially my father whose comments were the worst.

In Grade 9 I began steroid and Ayurvedic treatments. The vitiligo improved, but still the mocking continued. Nevertheless, I told myself that I would survive, and I would become good at something. I started to study hard and excel academically. I was on the honor role. Teachers really liked me, students started to ask me for help with their math homework. I'd turned into a nerd! I began altering the clothes that my mother bought me, making them my own fashion statement with a few stitches here and there. One year, I was nominated most fashionable!

At school, we had a liberal education, we were free to express ourselves and the kids would talk about their plans for the future, the university they wanted to go to. At home, I got the message loud and clear that *no* I would not be going to university! Instead, my father and mother would arrange a marriage for me or rather they would try. In truth, my father believed no one would want to marry me due to my vitiligo.

Meanwhile, I was becoming increasingly competent in the family business, doing the accounting and many more chores than my brother who had severe dyslexia. My father was aware I'd grown powerful and in response, he'd put me down. He'd tell me, "You're a woman, don't speak too much," don't be this, don't be that. Only a few years ago he actually admitted that he was afraid that my intellectual aptitude would make it difficult for them to find me a husband.

When I graduated secondary school, my international friends went off to university, but my Indian friends from the community in Lisbon, which had grown to about 4,000 by this time, stayed at home to help build family businesses. Even though I had become culturally mixed in my attitude – a Gujarati Indian girl living in Portugal and going to an American school – this is what I did too, I helped my parents in the family business. I'd also become a bit of a rebel, embracing my vitiligo with an attitude that was very Portuguese: "If you don't like it, don't look!"

I had promised my mother I would marry the man they chose for me and in fact I was glad of it. I desperately wanted to leave my parents' house, to get away from my father. My future husband had lived through the wars in Mozambique and then in 1989 he'd come on his own to Portugal to pursue a new life. My father had chosen someone for me that was just like him. I remember clearly that my mother said, "This proposal has come and you may not receive another, you have to accept this offer."

When my future husband came to visit, my mother told me, "Go and put on your *punjabi*" and "don't talk too much," which was a reference to the fact that I did talk a lot. I had grown in confidence – my father would send me to the banks and to the lawyers –I was not shy, on the contrary, I felt comfortable talking with just about anyone.

My parents took him to the sitting room, where a tray of sweets and tea was set for me to offer everyone present. My mother called to me to come and I did, but in my ripped jeans and T-shirt, and with no makeup so that my vitiligo was very visible. In I waltzed with my Valley Girl American attitude.

In our culture we have witnesses to meetings like this, so another young couple from the temple came by. I started talking with them, and then my future husband asked my parents if he could take me and the other young couple out for a coffee. The young couple, our chaperones, left us alone to walk in Belem. I turned to my future husband and said, "Look, I cannot cook, I have vitiligo, I'm very stubborn, my parents are not my best friends." I was very real about myself and very honest.

I accepted his offer of marriage, though I did not love him. He was 23 and I was 21.

When my engagement was announced in the Indian community there was some surprise. I was very well known. Often I was called upon to do some interpreting from Portuguese to English or some speaking or writing or interviews. I was an extrovert and my husband-to-be was nothing like me. Like my brother, he's dyslexic and consequently he hadn't studied much. We had nothing to talk about. We had nothing in common. And his family did not take to me. They saw me as a rebel. His sisters would criticize me, always implying that I was inept in trivial things such as cooking and housekeeping and they also believed they were superior in their religious knowledge. So I started to read the scriptures, and when they would criticize me, referencing the scriptures, I would say, "Where is it written?" Given that I could recite the Bhagavad Gita, I would be able to put them in their place.

When we were married, my husband and I started working together. We would fill up our van and travel around Portugal, selling our goods and products to retail stores. We did this for about a year and a half, and in 1993, we had an opportunity to go to Luanda. Angola was at war and our families did not want us to go as we had our first daughter by this time and she was only 4 months old. My husband suspected there'd be opportunities for us there, despite the war, or maybe because of the war, so he said, "We're going!"

The move to Luanda caused us to suffer a lot of hardships. Nevertheless, we were lucky to find the right business, a small shop, and we saved and saved and then we expanded, importing containers of our product, domestic electrics. Within a short period of time, we did really well. In fact, we flourished.

Despite how well we were doing, my husband would always disparage me, just like my father. The saving grace was my children. When I had my first daughter I was so happy and in love with my baby girl. I knew I would make it possible for her to pursue the opportunities that were denied me. We went on to have four girls, and during those years we were going back and forth between Angola and Portugal. In 2000 we went to Mozambique where we did really well in business. I found and joined an international women's group. I also studied homeopathy and Ayurveda, though

I was never able to practice. And my charity work included working with HIV patients. I had a life beyond the family and a lot more freedom and I was content.

My girls also did well. They were good students and I wanted them to have a well-rounded education, and they did. My eldest daughter went onto university in Switzerland, and the second daughter went to university in the U.K., attaining her Master's degree from King's College. I always nudged the girls forward, wanting the best for them.

There were a lot of social upheavals in Mozambique including kidnappings of families, who were then held captive for perhaps up to a month or more until ransoms were paid. This prompted us to move back to Portugal. In 2014 we arrived and moved into a beautiful home outside Lisbon in Sintra. Before we left Mozambique, we started a non-profit philanthropic organization called *Minhembeti,* an African word meaning "Tears." It's my husband's project since he wanted to leave a legacy behind. Given that he doesn't have a son to take his name, he thinks this project will carry his name into the future. Even though it's my husband's project, the girls and I are all involved. My husband is the president and I'm the vice president and we have a staff that manages the foundation and with whom we stay closely connected.

The foundation includes a hospital and a clean water project; it also supports a school and agriculture. I've lectured there regularly to the local women about the importance of protecting themselves against HIV. My girls were very involved with the "Toy Project" which teaches local women how to make stuffed African animals from *capulana,* the colorful fabric of Mozambique. The sale of these toys through the foundation subsequently supplies the women with an income.

In the Indian culture this kind of work through the foundation is *Seva* a Sanskrit word meaning "selfless work" which is carried out with no expectation of a return. It is done out of kindness and at the same time with the intention that it will contribute to the improvement of a community.

To this day, when my husband and I socialize with the Indian community and with his business-related partners here in Portugal, he still asks that I talk less, that I don't express all my opinions. This is the way it is, so I've learned how to be less than I am in certain situations.

It's difficult. I love to learn, but my husband is threatened by that, and also by the fact that I speak English and he does not. My capacity with language and communication certainly gives me entrée into many more interesting and exciting situations than my husband is comfortable with. During the day I do what I want, I quench my thirst for social and intellectual interactions with my Portuguese, Indian and international friends, but in the evening I am my husband's dutiful Indian wife.

I go twice a year to Mozambique. My husband travels even more these days, which for the girls and me is often the best time at home. My husband knows this. We do miss him, but we have more freedom when he's gone. He's created a secure family environment for us, and he's very generous. The girls have gone to the best schools and the two elder ones to the best universities abroad. They have had the opportunities that I did not have.

My eldest is in love and recently she became engaged. It won't be an arranged marriage.

My husband wanted her to marry a Brahmin. His family stressed the importance of the first born setting an example by marrying someone within the caste. But she fell in love with a young boy from a lower caste. My husband was very upset about this, but my daughter employed a very clever strategy when talking to her father. She said, "You know Dad, if you don't want me to marry him, I'll marry someone you choose, but I will never love that person." My husband knows that I do not love him, and he wanted his daughter to be happy, so after six months he relented.

My daughter will marry the boy she chose. Regardless, I've told her that life is a challenge, it won't all be a garden of roses, but she is strong, hard working and loving.

Where is she now?
Sandhya's permanent home and family is in Portugal. As I write, she's on one of her biannual visits to Mozambique, tending to the affairs of her and her husband's foundation.

Maria Salomão-Schmidt

Introducing Maria
Several summers back, Maria was in Portugal for her annual visit. We met through mutual international friends and I was immediately struck by her joy-filled personality. She's also a thoroughly entertaining woman: Maria has a way of injecting hip urban quips and pop-culture vernacular into every conversation while looking directly at you with arched eyebrows and a wickedly gorgeous grin that stretches ear-to-ear. When in her company, you simply cannot take anything too seriously, particularly yourself! Yet I discovered that underlying the fun and games she carries deep sorrow and loss, which she's quite comfortable talking about, and with the same level of passion and elation that infuses her every interaction.

In her words
I was born in Lisbon in a hospital that is now a Toyota dealership and my first job out of college was in Japan! When Mom was pregnant with my brother and I was 9-months old, Dad left. He went to America. After three years, he 'called for us to come'. There are things I remember, such as getting on the plane one week before my fourth birthday. I had three little dolls that someone had given me at the airport – I still have one of them – I was so excited for the big adventure that we were on together. When we arrived it was early morning, and I was in a strange place. But I did not remember my father; I didn't really know him.

My paternal grandmother came from up north where you were either a servant or you had a servant. Her mother died when she was young and her older sisters raised her. They were servants in the home of a wealthy family, and from age 6 this is where my grandmother was also a servant. My beloved grandmother was raped in her late teens, and the product was my father who was born out of wedlock, a huge disgrace, so she married anyone she could find, which happened to be the town drunk, a physically abusive man.

When Dad was a kid, he lived for 10 years in Casa Pia, a home for poor boys. I don't know much about his history there, other than it was a really tough time. My grandmother said that she would bring him food, but apparently he would never get it. In his early 20s, Dad was a professional soccer player in Portugal. He was a goalie for Benfica's farm team, but he was so aggressive – he broke someone's jaw – he got kicked out of the league.

My mom had had miscarriages before my brother and I were born. The conditions she lived with under the Salazar's regime were incredibly difficult. Many people don't realize that Amnesty International started as a result of the oppression in Portugal (*see footnote* [1]). Desperate for an answer that doctors could not provide, Mom agreed to go to a séance where she was advised of a solution that would help her carry a pregnancy to term. She was also very religious and every day she went to church to light a candle to Mary, promising that if she had a healthy baby it would be in honor of Mary. Ten months later I was born!

After we arrived in the U.S. we lived in Hudson, Massachusetts, which has a big Portuguese community, mainly from the Azorean islands. Because the immigrant thing to do was to

Americanize your name instead of Maria de Lourdes, I was called Marylou or Maria. I loved that community, but I was not happy at home. I wanted to leave and until I could do that, I learned by observing: Some girls got married or got pregnant just to get out, but that was not going to be me. Instead I escaped to the local library where I read voraciously, looking for answers, 'how do I do this, how do I do that?' I always wanted to know how I could disassemble emotional pain and painful life events.

Every summer we came back to Portugal. I love, love, loved coming back! We'd go to my aunt and uncle's home in Lisbon and in August we'd go to the Algarve. Portugal was always happy family time to me. These days when I return, my accent is totally east coast American, but when in conversation in my mother tongue with the Portuguese, they don't know that I've spent most of my life in America. When I'm in the U.S., I'm American and not obviously from anywhere else. But in Portugal I feel like I'm amongst my tribe.

I graduated from Boston College in 1989, majoring in Communications. I wanted to work in Public Relations (PR) but right about that time the economy tanked. I also wanted my 20s to be about travel and discovery so I considered going to England. I had a part-time job at a Japanese school, and decided why not Japan! I ended up spending a year there when I was 22. The language, the people, the food, I loved it all and I could see similarities between Japan and Portugal, such as the architecture. I saw buildings in Japan that I think look the same as buildings in Coimbra; probably the Japanese influence comes from the days of *The Discoveries*, when in the early 1500s the Portuguese were the first Westerners to enter Japan and trade.

After Japan, I went back to Massachusetts and got a job as a nanny. Because the guy I was nannying for was President of a big public relations firm, I also started to work in his company. But I wasn't making the kind of money I wanted to make so I decided to go back to school to get my Master's in business. I did the fast track program in two years, got a job offer in Boston earning a lot more money than I had previously, and then I was recruited to be Vice President for a PR firm in San Francisco doubling my Boston income!

Around this time it was clear Dad was having an affair, probably he'd been having affairs all along, but after I graduated college, we found out that he'd fathered a child with another woman. I was on a family vacation when my sister-in-law told me. I was so angry I yelled at my mother, "Have you no self-respect!" She'd stayed with him all that time! But my mom is a *good Catholic*.

Dad ended up marrying the woman he was having an affair with, and eventually I got to know her, she's only a year older than me, and actually she's lovely. She and Dad went on to have two more kids – I have a half sister who is 35-years younger than me. Fortunately, when I was in my late teens, Mom went back to school for an undergraduate degree in history, and then she also earned her Master's in Special Education, so by the time Dad remarried, she was able to support herself financially.

During my studies at Simmons Graduate School of Boston, my MBA program had a women's conference every year and Oprah spoke one year. I was her volunteer assistant for part of the conference. At a similar event when I was 27, I met Jane Goodall. God, talk about calm, she makes calm look erratic! I had my hair down, and she came up to me and asked, "Does anyone have a pen?" I was doing PR for the conference, so I said, "Ms. Goodall, I really love your work." And she said, "Oh what a sweet child," all the while stroking my long hair down the length of it, and I was like, "*Woo*, this is what she probably does with the chimps!"

My 30s and 40s were about family. When I first met my husband, he was pretty shut down emotionally, but he had other amazing qualities. He had a son by his previous marriage who lived with us every other week; he'd just turned 6 when Doug and I met. We then went on to have our first daughter, and 16-months later we had our second daughter, Sophia, who was born with Downs Syndrome.

Sophia died in my arms. Boom! She was gone! The paramedics came. We went to the hospital. All the while I was thinking 'she'll be okay, she's only 13-months old'. While Sophia was in Emergency, we waited till the doctor came to talk with us and when he did, he was incredibly mechanical saying "your daughter came in at 9:45 a.m. exhibiting signs of ..." and I interrupted asking, "Is she dead?" He repeated himself and I interrupted again. He snapped, "Don't interrupt me!" I started crying and screaming at which point he softened a bit and then he told us that Sophia was brain dead.

She was so sweet and so adorably cute you just wanted to eat her all up! She'd put up her arms to be lifted, and she had big, big, big blue eyes! That baby was liquid sunshine. This lifetime is so temporary and we make out like it's not. After Sophia died it was like everything was skewed. Everything that anyone had ever said to me vaporized. Nothing was real. Her death totally transformed us all.

My heart was so broken that I miscarried two subsequent pregnancies. We considered adopting a Portuguese baby, but we heard it was hard, and we didn't need hard, we needed flow, so we went through the Department of Social Services in the U.S. Our adoptive daughter was 18 months old at the time that we were going through the adoption process. And then I found out I was pregnant, which we didn't mention because I'd already miscarried that year and we thought I might again. Our adopted daughter's health was not good when she came to us, as her birth mother's cocaine use had affected her development in utero. Our last daughter arrived a couple of months later – my pregnancy had not miscarried.

Disheartened with PR, I'd changed careers and moved into real estate, eventually starting my own real estate brokerage. This allowed me to set my own schedule, take care of my family, and write a blog called ButterflyMoms. Inspired by Sophia it was inspirational writing, the sharing of wisdom with other moms. It grew to a weekly readership of two thousand. Even Oprah read it!

About a year before Oprah publicly announced that she was ending her show, my brother asked me to be godmother to his daughter. I went to Chicago to see my brother, and while there, I went to Oprah's corporate headquarters and TV production studios, but it was closed for production. The gift shop was open and I said to the staff, "I want to be on the Oprah show, what do I do?" The first person I talked with directed me to a page on O's website and said, "Just write your story in bullet points." I wrote my bullet points mentioning an Oprah show I'd seen 11 years previously in which a mother who'd lost her child had been asked what the gift of that loss was. I remarked that contemplating this question helped me through my darkest hours. A week later, O's people contacted me.

For the next year it was back and forth, back and forth. The sudden death of a Downs Syndrome baby is not a topic that fits in with just any show. I documented the whole thing on the ButterflyMoms blog. At one point I thought, "I'm going to *walk* to Chicago and get on that show!" Really, I was going to walk the thousand miles from Boston to Chicago, a pilgrimage in honor of my baby girl. But the producers said to me, "No, don't draw attention to your story like that, Oprah won't go for it."

The end of the year came around, and so too the taping of the very last Oprah show. I was sad, because it looked like my story was not going to be included. I called the producers and thanked them so much, for all they'd done, working hard on my behalf. They really were so kind. They'd let me live with the hope and the dream that I could share how Sophia's sudden death had inspired me to find the gifts in this tragic experience.

I wrote a post on ButterflyMoms, thanking everyone for their support, writing that I wasn't able to realize my dream. And the moment I pressed send, I got a call: "It's the Oprah Show, we'd like to set up an interview." It was a Friday when I got that call. They wanted to interview me the following day! I'm a working mom with four kids – busy, busy, busy – but I said, "Sure, I'm free!"

I had four interviews on the understanding that it might not mean anything. I was on pins and needles because they were taping for their last shows and no one had any idea what interviews they were going to use. The next day, Sunday, I was at a restaurant with my husband, and the phone rang. It was O's show again. They said, "We're going to use your piece, congratulations!"

I believe I was given the opportunity to share Sophia's story because I'd surrendered. I'd let go of my hopes and expectations and in the process, I learned that the lighter you are, the more you rise in your level of experience. It was a chance for me to really pay attention to the energy I put out, because what you put out determines what happens around you and where you find yourself.

There has been so much serendipity in my life, things happening for a reason and at the right time. I was often-times sad growing up in the U.S., but returning to my birthplace each summer, I'm aware that you have to leave and come back in order to appreciate what Portugal has to offer. I've never been any place in the world and felt the joy and heart energy that has always been available to me here and I want to be the soul that spreads that beautiful energy. My mission is to reduce suffering by bringing more love to our planet.

Now every summer I bring our teenage daughters, who are fluent in Portuguese, and they love Portugal just as I did as a kid. Doug knows I hate returning to Massachusetts after the summer, that's why we rent an apartment just outside Lisbon in Paço de Arcos year-round. Last year I came back in October for a couple of weeks on my own. This year it'll be a month, as I'm writing a book and I need time alone to do that.

Where is she now?

Maria wrote her book, *Finally Full of Yourself: Unlocking Your Spiritual DNA* and successfully launched it on Amazon where it hit the 'top 100 books on Happiness'! It is one of a number of her professional offerings as a Transformational Life Coach helping people 'ignite their Soul's purpose'. She's still based in Massachusetts and continues to spend summers in Portugal where she has run, and is planning on running again, her "Happy Me" spiritual retreats.

www.coachmemaria.com

Footnote 1:

"Amnesty International began with one man's outrage and his courage to do something about it. After learning of two Portuguese students imprisoned for raising a toast to freedom in 1961, British lawyer Peter Benenson published an article, "The Forgotten Prisoners" in the Observer newspaper. That article launched the "Appeal for Amnesty 1961", a worldwide campaign that provoked a remarkable response. Reprinted in newspapers across the world, his call to action resonated with the values and aspirations of people everywhere. This was the genesis of Amnesty International." Amnesty.org.uk.

Eva Sarmiento Fernández

Introducing Eva

Eva and I live in the same apartment complex. I met her through a mutual Portuguese friend in 2014. I wondered why Eva had crossed the border from Spain to live on the coast here, after all Spain is a wonderful country with fabulous beaches, diverse landscapes, vibrant culture and great food. Tall and elegant, Eva has a trending Madrid style suggestive of a former model or someone who'd worked in fashion. Contrary to my impression of her, thrice weekly, she meets up with her colleagues at local children's hospitals, puts on a round, rubbery red nose, oversized funny shoes and clothes she's found at the local gypsy market. And together, she and her professional Red Nose Clowndoctor colleagues bring joy and sunshine to an otherwise grey environment, brightening the lives of kids with cancer and other serious illnesses. Behind the scenes, things weren't all sunny and joyful: The clowndoctor company she worked for had management issues. I learned that Eva's dream was to break away at some point and create her own project.

In her words

I had my first travel experience when I was five. I went with my mother and brother to Helsinki, Finland, two years in a row for a three-month summer holiday, and even at that young age the trip stimulated my curiosity. It showed me that the world is a very big place.

My mother had a Finnish boyfriend who paid for our trips. The first time we went by train from Madrid to Paris. It was a beautiful train with all the amenities. From Paris we traveled to the coast and from there we took a boat, spending a night on board where I had my first experience of a buffet. So much delicious food! It was all very, very exciting and different to a child from Madrid. To this day, I remember all the smells and flavors of that trip.

At 19, I was an exchange student at a high school in California. I learned English, picking it up in school and at home with the family I lived with. It was a private exchange with a family my mother knew. The mother was a high school teacher and the father a physicist. While I was with them, their daughter went to stay with my mother in Madrid.

My English really improved when I met my American boyfriend. Ryan and I traveled around together after I left my family and before I came back to Spain. I had the kind of freedom in America that I would never have had in Madrid. I'm genuinely grateful to my mother for this opportunity. She was very supportive, opening up my world so I could grow through these experiences abroad. I think because of my mother I developed a love of travel. I'd work to save money and I'd put it away, and then I'd break the piggy bank and take a trip, visiting places like Greece, Italy, France, the Czech Republic, Turkey, Brazil, Guatemala, the Congo and just recently, Uganda.

My work with those in need began on a whim when I was 21, in love, and ready for another adventure abroad. My boyfriend at the time and I volunteered with an agency that gave food to the homeless on the streets of Madrid.

We both then applied to a Catholic agency to do relief work in Africa. They asked me lots of questions such as what I'd studied, and what languages I could speak, which at that time were Spanish, English, French (and now I can add Portuguese to that list). The nuns at the agency told me, "Providence has sent you to us!" Apparently they were able to use my skills with language immediately. They asked about my boyfriend and his language skills, but he didn't speak French or English. "Not a problem," they said, "he will learn French."

Within weeks of applying, we were sent to a small village in the Congo. Crazy nuns! You know, they sent us without vaccines, without anything really. It's not that they were desperate for help they just didn't know what was appropriate. So in the late 1980s my boyfriend and I found ourselves in the Congo, in a small village where there were three cars: the nuns' car, the priest's car and the car for the Doctors Without Borders. As we got to know the sounds of the engines of each car, we knew who was coming. There I taught French to little girls as young as 5 years old.

This was another highly impactful trip, as I discovered another way *to be* in Africa. The culture is so different and obviously in a small village it was very different from the city of Madrid. I liked all these differences, particularly the small African village way of life.

After six months, I went back to Madrid and discovered another organization that placed volunteers abroad, working for them in the Central America Department in Madrid. I wanted them to eventually send me to Central America and actually, that's what happened. I was sent to Guatemala where I understood I'd be for a year and a half. The project was teaching writing and reading to adults and I had a paid administrative role. After one month, it didn't work out and I was sent back to Spain. I was young and naïve and that it didn't work out disappointed me enormously.

At 25, I started working in television. I had studied to be an international secretary and at a TV station in Madrid, I was in administration in the legal department. I was processing the film purchase contracts. I've always been curious so I took on more work, which included short film contracts, and then I started to do all the contracts for documentaries, and major American films, plus other film projects the company was taking on.

I was handling a lot, particularly in the legal department, and that was where I met the father of my kids, a lawyer. Soon after we met, I became pregnant. We weren't in love, but we were attracted. He said he wouldn't leave me. In fact, he really wanted to be a father. I thought, "Wow this guy is special." I was 29.

I always loved drama. When I was a kid, I wanted to be an actress, but my mother didn't support me. I had started to do workshops the year before I became pregnant, such as "Introduction to Theater" and clown workshops, which I actually did not like. I did these workshops for two years and then the year before we came to Portugal, I discovered theatrical improvisation or improv, as it's known, and I loved it. It was my kind of theater.

I came to Portugal from Madrid. The father of my children was not happy in Spain. I suggested to him that we come, and fortunately he found a good job here. Once we arrived, I had the idea that I was now closer to the rest of the world and I imagined it would be a springboard to somewhere or something else.

When we arrived, I knew no one. In Spain I had always done some sort of volunteer work so I looked for volunteer opportunities. I hoped it would connect me to the community. I asked the lady I bought my bread from, and anywhere else I struck up conversations, if anyone knew of any projects. Eventually I met a woman, a judge, who'd started a project to help women in jail. My volunteer work required that I go regularly to the jail to be with the interned, and sit and listen to these women who had children at home.

I had my own young kids at home. And one day when I took one of the boys to the hospital, I saw the work that clowndoctors do with sick kids – theater and social work all in one. I called the organization as I wanted to work with them, but they told me I couldn't. I was not a professional clown, and they weren't looking for anyone.

I came across them again one year later, when I went to the hospital for a check up. Again, I called them. This time they were looking for clowns. I was in the right place at the right time. They asked me to send in my CV. I think all my experience as a volunteer, both abroad and in Spain where I volunteered with the Red Cross, my theater studies, and the fact that I'd also studied the rights of children with UNICEF, helped me to get an interview.

There was a woman and a man, and two chairs at the interview. I thought, "I'm going to sit close to the woman."

She asked, "So you're a clown and you're husband is a lawyer," and I said, "Well he's a lawyer but I'm not a clown!" And she said, "Like me! We are twin souls!" She said this in the first interview. I think she was almost too nice. And then I left.

I passed that first interview and they asked me back to participate in three days of clown workshops. Even though it cost money and I was anxious that I wouldn't be able to do it, I didn't have anything to lose. At one point during the workshop, I was asked to do an improv story in front of an audience, and a clown skit too. Everyone laughed! It must have been good, as I got the job. A year into the clown work at the hospital, I had enough income to leave my relationship. My boys were 4 and 6 and I was able to launch my career as a clown, and my role as a single mother.

My clown mentor, and boss at work, died four years ago from cancer. Her death was one of a number of changes happening in my life at that time and though my work had given me cohesiveness during all the changes, I began to question whether I was on track.

During this period of uncertainty, I focused on writing my own one-woman shows and I also began performing them independently. And then I realized I just needed a break. I needed respite from the disappointment I felt over the politics at work, from my clowndoctor work, and from mothering.

My kids went to their father's, which was good. Teenage boys need to spend more time with their father, it's important for their development. I was also looking for perspective, for a sense of the bigger picture. In November 2015, I went to Uganda for two months with a Spanish project called "In Movement." A Spanish woman founded it and I proposed that I come and volunteer. It was the last of their summer projects as they were closing after eight years of operation. She agreed and I paid for my airfare and my lodgings. This made sense to me. If I'm a Western woman and I want to have an adventure, stepping out of my regular life to get some perspective, I don't think it's fair to charge the organization for my time, and in truth, everything is cheaper in Uganda and thus I could afford it.

In Uganda I worked alongside teachers working with the young people of the neighborhood in a program that was like a school activity. I worked mostly with young boys that were going to be classroom monitors. I offered clown workshops. It was the first time that I'd done something like this; even so, it was clear to me that it needed to be fun for the boys. And they had so much fun! Play, fun and humor are human experiences that cross culture and borders.

The professional part of my day was very stimulating and it gave my time structure, and I met and worked with these wonderful young people, making some lovely friends along the way. It was very important to me to also have a personal experience, and it came to me when I met a wonderful young woman. Maybe 24 or 25 years old, Mirembe is English and Ugandan, a real African beauty. She showed me an amazing garden, a permaculture project close to Lake Victoria. I ended up spending a lot of time there. I found it so impressive.

When I returned from Uganda I went back to my clown-doctor work and the problems in the company. I wasn't happy and I realized that I needed to make a big change.

It took another year for me to ask for a meeting with my employer to say I was leaving the company. During that year I was working with some clown friends developing a project, specifically Social Clown work, it's also called Relational Clown work.

Despite how unhappy I'd been with the company I'd worked with, I still loved my work as a clown. So from January to June 2016 my friends and I developed a Social Clown project. We intended to take it into homes for the elderly to stimulate, entertain, engage and motivate the residents.

By September 2016, we had seven people on the team and we found a film company that agreed to help us by making a promotional video of our work. In October we were put in contact with a journalist who wrote about us, and from there the media has been in contact with us, which resulted in a television interview that was subsequently aired.

I'm a little bit tired of seeing myself everywhere, well I'm not actually everywhere, but I mean it's weird for me to see all the pictures and the videos full of images of me.

I would like to see this project take off and be a success. By success, I don't mean that I want to be constantly traveling here and there. I don't want to do any more big trips for now, unless I'm traveling as an artist, as a clown, to comedy festivals around the country, which I'd love to do. I want the project to involve talented professionals so that it grows into something that I can be proud of. I want it to be a project that has integrity, where the clowns talk honestly and openly with one another about building our project together. I want it to offer my colleagues and me the work that we love doing, and I also want it to allow me to have work-life balance so that I have time to develop my own personal projects.

I have two shows that I've been working on, performing and refining, a short show called *Evarista* about aging, and a longer one *Ooo La La*, about a Spanish Flamenco dancer. However, my focus now is on making this social clown project a success.

I know I've grown creatively from the clowndoctor work and it's exciting to see where I might be able to take it all. Years ago I did a clown workshop during which my teacher defined clown work as important. Clowns teach us that we are not perfect, that we don't always do things well, but despite this, we still have the right to be happy, and we need to laugh at ourselves. Clowns give us this chance, we laugh at their antics but, in fact, we are laughing at our own stupidity and messiness, at our humanness.

Where is she now?
I don't see Eva very much these days. She's busy at her desk dealing with paperwork and funding applications and a myriad of other details involved in growing her social clown project, *A Vista*. I do periodically see Eva in the promotional videos she mentioned. More recently on Facebook, I saw publicity for a Sunday afternoon family dance with a live band on the streets of an inner-city neighborhood in Lisbon. It was accompanied by an image of Eva and her team of clowns dancing with the elderly. There's a great deal of humanity in social clown work, and it's beautiful to see it in action. *www.avisita.pt*

Esther Schenkel

Introducing Esther

I was at a party in Cascais, a dinner to which Esther had also been invited, when with a bit of encouragement from the hostess, she got up from the table and spontaneously sang. On hearing her rich and deeply powerful voice, I secretly thought with her look and that voice, she could've been a rock star! Instead she found her way into the healing arts, as a teacher, coach and workshop facilitator, and this is the context in which I first came to know her. Esther and a colleague were offering a daylong women's empowerment workshop in Cascais, and though I had been to many such events in the U.S., I hadn't sampled any in Portugal. As it turned out, I partnered with Esther in a number of the experiential exercises that day, learning quite a bit about her, including how open, warm and large hearted she is, and how she also loves to dance!

In her words

We lived in The Hague until I was 6 and then we moved to Zoetermeer, "Sweet Lake City" in English. We had huge grounds outside where my two younger sisters and I could play freely with all the kids from the neighborhood. From a very young age I took dancing classes in classical ballet, tap, jazz, ballroom, rock & roll and Latin. Music and dance were a big part of my growing up. I also wanted to sing but the message from my family was that it was not for me.

Nevertheless, at various times I took singing classes but I never seriously pursued it. I also learned the flute, but stopped, even though I really enjoyed it.

Two or three times a year we'd go on a family vacation, often camping. My parents didn't have much money, but their attitude was "even if we have to sit on boxes, we're going on vacation." So that's what we did. My parents had a very active social life with their friends, a group of about 15 to 20 couples, and we'd all spend holidays together. I have such happy memories of those good times: camping in summer, playing outside, learning other languages, particularly French as we sometimes camped in France.

In contrast to these wonderful childhood summers, in primary and secondary school I was bullied a lot. And at home, I had a very difficult adolescence when my parents tried to contain my self-expression. I felt like I had to fight for the right to be me. Perhaps it was because of this, or perhaps it was just my destiny, but by 15, I wanted to leave the Netherlands, and within a few years, I did.

At 17, I began my bachelor's in Human Resources (HR) and I remember thinking "now life really begins." I wanted to be a physiotherapist, but I didn't have physics, so I couldn't do it. Instead, I did HR, like my father. While studying for my bachelor's, I worked in an Italian restaurant twice a week and once I finished my studies, I continued working but at an employment agency, madly saving my money. I was determined to leave Holland and go to Italy. I knew the Italian owner of the restaurant really well and as a result of my friendship with him, my plan was to go to Florence. Plus, I loved hearing spoken Italian. It's such a beautiful language, it sings and it dances.

At the point at which I was ready to give up my jobs and the apartment I was living in, I went to my parents and told them of my "Italy plan." They didn't like the idea, suggesting that I go on vacation to Italy instead.

I was 21 when I left Holland for Italy. I was desperate to learn the language and even though I didn't know anyone, I found a one-month program at a language school with classes in the morning, and with enrolment came lodging. I shared an apartment with a Danish and an American girl. After the month was up, I needed to leave. The other girls were staying on. I stayed illegally in the apartment until I was found out and asked to leave. It was terribly upsetting. I sat in front of the door to the apartment and cried, wondering what to do.

I was determined to stay in Italy, so I went through the laborious task of applying for a work permit. In those days there were borders. There wasn't a European Union. Fortunately, the work permit came through and I found a good-paying job. For the next year, I shared a house with four Italian girls and I had a great time, exploring and learning the language while living in Florence.

In Holland people like to put you in a box, and I don't like boxes and borders. Leaving Holland was a way of breaking free for me. When you live somewhere for a long period, people have expectations saying things like, "But that's not you, that's not who you are." By leaving, I could be me, without people telling me who they thought I was or how I should behave.

Leaving gave me the emotional freedom that I needed in order to grow into the person I was meant to become.

I flourished in Italy. I would write long letters to my parents telling them just that. By this time, we had a close relationship and we communicated well. The owner of the apartment I was renting with the other girls wanted me to commit to another year's lease. I wasn't willing to do that. And yet when I left, I had no idea of the next step.

My parents had some family friends who were from the Caribbean and who'd lived in Holland for the past 20 years. Around the time I moved out of the apartment in Italy, they were moving back to St. Martin, a half-French half-Dutch island in the Caribbean. I had gone there for five weeks when I was 19 and now three years later, I decided to go back again.

I was planning on staying three months with the intention of then traveling through the U.S. However, I got a job in a bar and I started to meet people and make friends. Life happened and I just went with the flow. From my work in a bar, I transitioned to working in a Government position. I discovered that the Afro-Caribbeans had a very different work ethic, which made the office environment challenging. For instance, I would do my work and meet my deadlines. That's what the Dutch do! But I had a colleague who questioned this with, "Who are you trying to impress!" It was clear she was threatened by my efficiency, so I would let my work pile up, until someone questioned that, and then I'd start working efficiently again.

My work life on St. Martin was not great but I had a lot of fabulous friends who saw me through many big life lessons. They were like family to me. We were always at the beach either diving, swimming, or sailing. The island was filled with people of different nationalities: Russians, Canadians, Americans, Europeans; it seemed like every country was represented. There was this wonderful mix of people, language and culture.

But St. Martin has an underbelly: its nickname is "Pirate Island," people come to make money and not pay taxes. There was a lot of corruption and in that sense it was sometimes compared to African countries. It also felt as though people weren't really invested in the island, rather, they were there to use it for their own benefit. For these reasons, I didn't want to stay, but I ended up staying five years, until I was 26.

Once again, I wasn't sure of the next step. I did know that I wanted to learn Spanish this time.

I asked amongst my friends if anyone knew of someone who lived in a Spanish-speaking country. I was thinking Spain, Mexico or Argentina. It was my dad who said, "I know someone in Chile." Initially I rejected that proposal. Chile didn't sound exciting to me. It turned out that these people my father knew were a Chilean couple that had moved back to Chile after living for 20 years in Holland. They spoke Dutch and Spanish and they were good people. I did go to Chile in the summer of 1997 and stayed with them for three months. They left while I was there to visit family in Columbia and I ended up learning Spanish out of a book and by immersing myself in the language.

During the eighteen months I spent in Chile, I went north to Antofagasta, near the Atacama Desert, where I worked in a restaurant and met a guy who came from a village in the south. We traveled together to his village, Villarica, which is situated in an area of beautiful green mountains and volcanoes, and there I found another job. While in the south, I sailed for a couple of weeks through the canals of Magallanes. These waterways separate mainland South America to the north and Tierra del Fuego to the south. I also sailed down to Puerto Williams, a town located on Isla Navarino facing the Beagle Channel. I flew to Ushuaia, the capital of Tierra del Fuego, and Punta Arenas, Chile's southernmost region. I met a couple of Americans who said they were going to the Carretera Austral where there is no public transportation. They were going by car and I asked if I could come along. We camped together for a couple of weeks.

Chile was an immersive working and traveling experience. It helped me become fluent in Spanish, certainly it was not about making money; I made very little and the cost of living was high. Actually, I realized how blessed we are in countries like Holland where you can always return to good wages and the comforts of life.

I came to the realization that it was time for a different experience: one with less financial struggle. I called my father and asked if he could buy me a ticket so I could fly back to Holland. He did that without question. I'd been gone most of my 20s and I knew my parents wanted me home. And at 30, having spent almost eight years abroad learning and growing through travel, I was ready to be back in my country meeting the challenges there that would cause me to grow in a different way.

In Holland, everyone I knew had a house, a car and a family. I moved back in with my parents with just a suitcase. That was not easy, but it was an interesting period, getting to know my parents again. Living away from one another for so long, you lose track of each other's development – my parents had aged, and no doubt they recognized the huge personal changes I'd gone through.

I stayed eight months before settling into my own apartment and a new job with the U.N. at The Hague, working at the International Criminal Tribunal for the former Yugoslavia. It was an administrative job and thus the work was not so interesting. I worked for the Facility Management Team taking care of the entire building. I had come into this position from an international environment and from traveling and working abroad, so now finding myself back in my country but in an international environment, made me happy. People from all over the world worked there. I met people from the Middle East – Iranians and Israelis; and heard stories of people who had been through war struggles in places like East Timor. It was eye opening. I stayed with the Tribunal for a year. All the while wanting more enriching work.

Friends from St. Martin who had also returned to Holland, were working for Deloitte and Touche, a big finance consulting company. I applied for a position in the Human Resources department. They hired me and I began working in various governmental offices in different cities. After a couple of years, I had the "rotating door" experience, which meant I quit and they hired me back as a consultant. Within days of starting up as a consultant, 9-11 happened in New York and the economy tanked.

On the side, I had been doing a year-long program to train trainers in neuro-linguistic programming, and I was also doing a three-year training in energy healing. This was a self-development path that I was easily able to finance with my income.

Out of the blue, I got a call. It was a job offer back in St. Martin. I said, "Yes," but I negotiated that I'd fly back to Holland every six-to-eight weeks. I'd enrolled in another self-development training and I wanted to complete the program. I was about 37.

I was planning on staying one year and once again I stayed longer, in fact, I stayed seven years. During this time, I partnered with a woman from the Antilles who offered workshops in Curaçao, an island in the southern Caribbean Sea north of the Venezuelan coast. Together we did training workshops on how to recruit and do interviews, and also workshops on personal leadership for women. I went back and forth between Curaçao and St. Martin where I was also doing projects for the government, and consulting as a behavioral instructor at a medical university. I also started to do massages. St. Martin attracted the rich and famous and sometimes I did massages on multi-million dollar yachts, which was unreal. The biggest tip I received was around $100!

The "yachting scene" was a very artificial world. Apple's Steve Jobs periodically had a huge yacht anchored in the harbor. The amount of money I'd see floating in front of me in the harbor was mindboggling, while in a back street of the town, living in a tiny shack, there'd be 10 Haitians trying to survive and make enough money to send back to Haiti.

I left St. Martin for the second time. My father had cancer and I felt I needed to be closer to home. With my father's death, I began to think about what was important to me, what I wanted for myself, and where I wanted to be. What I realized is my community of close and heartfelt friends in Europe is of primary importance.

I was 44 when I returned to Europe from St. Martin. And in 2013 I did a workshop in Portugal. It was Personal Leadership for Women using the Enneagram. I knew people here who had lived in St. Martin; one owns a restaurant in Cascais just outside Lisbon. I stayed another month after the workshop finished and helped my friend build up her restaurant, which she had just bought.

One day I went for a jog and realized that I felt relaxed and at peace, more importantly, I felt grounded here. In many ways, Portugal or rather Cascais, which is where I spend most of my time, is the opposite to the energy of St. Martin where I was always pumped up and on the go, buzzed and busy, busy, busy! I ended up partnering with my friend. Given that the restaurant's clientele is international tourists the natural extension was a Bed & Breakfast, which I opened and operated, and together we promoted the two businesses.

Opportunities sometimes just need to arise organically and this one did and I jumped in with my eyes wide closed! I started the B&B in 2014. The first summer was very success-ful. I offered retreats, such as yoga weekends as well as one-day workshops and weeklong events and between my friends in Europe, and my friend's network through the restaurant, I did well. In the winter it was quiet, with few winter guests and the house was impossible to heat. This turned into a major problem.

My business relationship with my restaurateur friend ended, and I was on my own. Ultimately it was best for me to operate my business independently. On the plus side, my social life picked up. I made new friends, and I started to build a life for myself in Portugal. Unfortunately the B&B business folded, but it served its purpose: it got me out of St. Martin.

It's hard to admit but the choices I've made always gave me a bit of an adrenaline rush. I loved being on the rollercoaster of life. It made me feel alive. I'm ready for a change now, and that's what I feel Portugal offers me. I've made a decision to put down roots here, which is unusual for me, given that I seem to have some self-judgment around "settling down." Now in my late-40s it's what I want to do. I need to stop trying to be everywhere and just be here.

And with settling, I want to bring in a relationship. I've always thought about relationships like this: "if they're there, they're there, if they're not, that's fine," which is a reflection of the fact that I was not always there – I mean if you're always moving, you're hard to find. I've never been married so perhaps a significant relationship will be a part of the next chapter. If not, what I learned from my father is the importance of community and friends and that's what I try to foster in my life, no matter where I am.

Where is she now?

Esther spent months after her B&B folded looking for new opportunities in and around Lisbon and Cascais. Despite a number of leads, nothing opened up for her. She was incredibly discouraged, given her plan to establish herself here, but it was not meant to be. In 2016, she returned to The Hague. These days she has her own business in the Netherlands as a coach, trainer and teacher. *www.wisdomofthebody.eu* She tells me she still feels she doesn't quite belong there, she also said that that feeling eased upon reading a Maya Angelou quote: "*You are only free when you realize you belong no place – you belong every place – no place at all! The price is high, the reward is great.*"

Penny Imrie

Introducing Penny

Penny is one of the Sintra hikers I met when I first moved to Portugal and joined IWP. More than four years on, I periodically see her and it has become very apparent to me that one of her obvious loves is the color red. Whether it features in a kerchief tied around her neck, on her sunhat and matching handbag, or on a smart sweater or shirt, and always in her shade of lipstick, Penny accessorizes with red. Red really suits her. It matches her wonderfully warm and generous personality. For this reason, I'm drawn to Penny, her vitality is infectious. When we sat down to do her interview, I had already deduced from her appearance, and her fluency with several Latin languages, that she's a cultured woman who has moved in sophisticated circles and urban environments in South America and in a number of European countries. Certainly that was part of her story, but by no means all of it.

In her words

I have this image of my father donning a 1930s white suit and heading off into the jungle. It's a romantic notion, but still, I think my father was enormously courageous taking a job in Recife, northeast Brazil.

He came from quite a poor, humble family in Manchester and at a young age, he started working in a chartered accountant's office doing all the errands. His mentors were two elderly accountants who took a liking to him and as a result, they sent him to night school and Dad ended up becoming a chartered accountant. I know my father dreamt of a world beyond Manchester so as soon as he had his qualifications, he applied for a job he'd seen advertised in the paper. The job was with Deloitte, an accountancy firm with a long history in Brazil.

He came back to England some years later and married my mother who was also from Manchester. He took her back to Recife, but she hated it. She just couldn't come to terms with it. Nevertheless, she learnt Portuguese, though it was what I'd call kitchen Portuguese – in other words, only the maids could understand her.

My older brother was born in Recife, after which my father changed jobs and went to São Paulo where he was chief accountant with a big Brazilian export company. I was born and grew up in São Paulo and until the age of 13, I attended a British School called St. Paul's. As is the custom in good British families I was then sent to boarding school in the U.K., but I was, of course, accustomed to Brazilian culture: I spoke Portuguese (and English) and my friends were Brazilian. I did not like the British boarding school experience and I did everything I could to get out of it. Fortunately, I would travel back to Brazil most holidays. My brother, who is five years older than me, and who went to boarding school at 9, only traveled back once a year, consequently, we didn't grow up together.

I returned to Brazil after finishing my O levels and eventually did a secretarial course and a French course. When I was 18, my father retired and my parents moved to Portugal.

I went with them, though shortly thereafter I was dispatched to Paris for a year of finishing school. Each term we'd go somewhere, such as one term in Grenoble, another term in the south of France – my French improved to the point of fluency. After the year, I returned to Portugal and took my A Levels in Portuguese, French and English. I scraped through and with the help of my father got a job in London where I worked for two years at The Bank of London and South America, which was then taken over by Lloyd's Bank. I was a receptionist and interpreter helping people from South America who couldn't speak English.

I lived in a flat with six English girls. I'd get up and shower every day. After about a week a bossy flatmate said, "And how long do you expect to be having a shower everyday Penny?" I didn't realize the other girls weren't showering daily. "We have three baths a week," she said, suggesting that if I were going to shower so often then I should pay more rent per week.

After a couple of years in London, I wanted a change. I was working to save all my money to travel somewhere sunny for my two-week annual holiday. I loved the city, but I couldn't stand the cold, dark winters. I talked with a friend from Brazil who, like me, was living in London. Together, we managed to find jobs in southern Portugal.

That was in 1972, just after my 21st birthday. My father had given me a car, a little Mini-Minor that I called *Gordinha* – she was small and fat. A friend Melody, and I, and another friend from the bank, Claire, set off from London in *Gordinha*. Claire didn't last long. She missed her boyfriend so she left us in France. Mel and I continued. We drove to Albufeira, which was a little fishing village back then. We'd arranged to work for an Irish woman who had maybe five or six guest villas, and we'd stay in whichever villa was empty and help her run things. Mel was in the office and I was the "Cordon Bleu" cook. My first customers were orthodox Jews, but not only was I *not* a Cordon Bleu cook, I also knew nothing about kosher cooking. Despite my shortcomings, I stayed for the summer.

Before leaving London, I'd applied for lots of other jobs. I was delighted to receive notification that one of my applications had been accepted with an offer of a job out of Miami on the "Song of Norway" the Royal Caribbean Cruise lines first cruise ship. I was a Purserette, a female Purser or complaints officer, the person to whom guests came to lodge a comment or complaint.

All the girls on the ship were English – presumably we were cheap labor – and the officers were Norwegian. The guests would get off on Saturday morning and the new guests would board the ship in the afternoon. From Miami we sailed to Nassau in the Bahamas, the U.S. Virgin Islands, and San Juan, Puerto Rico, and then back to Miami. We wore a uniform all the time, except when in our cabin. I had a tiny cabin that was right on top of the motor to myself, but only because the girl I was initially sharing it with took off with an officer fairly quickly.

It was my first time in the United States and I learned so much about Americans. In Brazil we looked to America not Europe, to me Americans were the ones with money, the worldly ones, which I discovered was not entirely true. The first time someone on the cruise asked me where they could see the

Dolphin's game, I thought they were talking about dolphins in the water, but of course it was the Miami Dolphins, the football team! And I heard this all too frequently, "Please say something Miss, you've got such a cute accent!" I lasted one year on the "Song of Norway."

Without a job or money or any clue about what I was going to do, I went to visit my older brother in Panama. He had married an Ecuadorian girl and they had two young boys. The language in their home was Spanish, and while there, I picked up rudimentary Spanish by communicating with my nephews. My brother worked in Colon, the Free Zone in Panama where a lot of companies import and package their goods – it's a sort of tax haven – before exporting to Latin America and the States.

My brother set up a job interview for me with Christian Dior perfumes. It was a disaster, but the next interview with Chanel Perfumes as a sales rep was successful. The job involved traveling to Central and South America, the Caribbean, the U.S. and Canadian airports. The perfumes were imported already bottled, and assembled for merchandising by being packaged, labeled, and put into boxes. My first trip was to Central America in the '70s, when there was a lot of unrest, mostly in Nicaragua. Luckily I traveled to South America without issue. I was very well looked after, always met by a distributor, and put up in the best hotels.

Ian, the man I eventually married, worked for British America Tobacco (BAT) as their Panamanian marketing manager. He was English, born in London, but he'd spent most of his life in Latin America. When we met he was married, but the marriage was breaking down so sometimes they'd separate and then he would housesit for international friends on leave. His wife continued to live in the apartment that BAT rented for them (it actually belonged to Margot Fontaine, the ballerina, who was married to a Panamanian).

On one occasion, I was at the home where Ian was to housesit for mutual friends. They'd offered me their stationary exercise bike. Ian helped me home with the exercise bike, which I never used, except to hang clothes on. Ian was still married. It was clear he needed to sort his life out before we got involved. I was busy with my work, on the road three weeks out of four, traveling to airport Chanel outlets to train sales girls. My record was something like 14 airports in 12 days. I traveled so much I never spent a consecutive month at home. As a result, I never became a resident of Panama. It was a tiring and lonely life, though I learned how to be my own best company.

In early 1981, Ian was transferred to Nicaragua. We joked at the time, "The good news is you're General Manager; the bad news is it's Nicaragua."

He went to Managua, the capital city of Nicaragua, with the idea that his divorce would soon come through, and that I would leave Chanel, join him, and we'd get married. Despite the unrest, I felt I could cope with Nicaragua. I could speak the language and I understood the culture. Also the revolution was just over when Ian was transferred there.

Nicaragua had been under Somosa, the dictator, for 40 years. The Sandinista revolutionaries ousted him, taking control by the early '80s. Once the Sandinistas were in power, they also took control of all the big companies, mainly because

Somosa had shares in companies like Coco-Cola, the Rum Factory, and Flor de Caña. BAT never went to bed with the Somosa government so the Sandinistas had no shares in the tobacco company. It ended up that in our circle of friends, Ian was the only one working for a big corporation. Everyone we knew was either a diplomat or working for UNICEF, the U.N. or other aid programs.

Ian's divorce did come through and as we'd planned, I resigned from my seven-year career with Chanel and joined him in Managua where we married.

Due to Ian's corporate job, there were times when we felt scared, such as the days around July 19, Independence Day. The celebrations were broadcast on TV and we thought BAT would be taken over, but we concluded that the Sandinistas gained more from BAT running their company and generating the 85-90 percent tax revenue from the sale of cigarettes. Despite the fact that the revolutionaries were in power, initially I found it all quite novel: I was in my early 30s (Ian was 24 years older), and I was happily married with two young boys.

We lived in a house surrounded by a big fence and we had a gardener who carried a gun. Actually, everyone had a gun! There was a lot of fighting in the north, because of the Contras, the U.S. backed anti-Sandinistas. Every week there was someone at BAT who had someone near to them who had been killed. I chose not to go to the funerals, but each morning I prayed that nothing would happen to my family.

We had a big swimming pool and I taught my kids to swim before they could walk. You couldn't take children for a walk in the park; there was no park. There wasn't anywhere to walk, absolutely nowhere. Swimming was one of the things we could do. When my second son was born, I started teaching swimming. I set up a swimming school for mums and their babies. I taught every morning, every day. It kept me busy.

Food was rationed and as "head of the household" I'd go to the market on a weekly basis to collect our allocation of black market staples: rice, sugar, oil, beans, and coffee mixed with chicory. I was driving to the market one morning with the kids in the back seat when a policeman stopped the car with the intention of taking me to the police station. I started to cry and in between my sobs, I told him that he must let me go. Usually, if anything happened and obviously this was before mobile phones, I'd get word to Ian and he'd send someone to help. Despite things like this, we were actually very well looked after.

We held British passports, but we always spoke Spanish. It was rare that Ian and I spoke English, and even then only if we were in a room on our own. We worried people might assume we were American and in Nicaragua you wouldn't want to be singled out as American.

Periodically the boys and I would visit a friend in Miami. The kids were on my passport. An immigration officer stopped me once saying, "You're not allowed to have your children on your passport anymore." I said, "I'm coming into Miami in the middle of the night and you're telling me this now, *after* they let us get on the plane to come here?" And he said, "You telling me my job ma'am?" And I said, "Okay, well you keep my kids!" I was so angry! I walked away leaving the boys standing at the counter. He yelled after me, "Okay but next time." Returning to Nicaragua was worse. It was all very communist, with mirrors behind us. If I made an error filling out the landing card, I'd have to fill out another and go back to the end of the line.

The company had a lake house and a beach house and Ian and I rented a house in San Juan del Sul, a town on the southwest coast. On these weekends away we made some great friends such as President Dona Violeta Chamorro. To date, she is the only female president of Nicaragua and she's also the politician who eventually became known for ending the Contra wars. Violeta had a house next to us at the beach and the boys went to school with her grandchildren. At school, the Instituto Espanol, the kids learnt to count in Spanish with picture books filled with *pistolas*, they also sang revolutionary songs about Carlos Fonseca, the Nicaraguan hero.

We'd throw company parties at which we'd also have to wine and dine the Sandinistas. They loved my crystal glasses and our French brandy. I became very cynical living with this. They did do some good, mainly in education, but in the end they abused their power. Nobody liked the Sandinistas, but many years later they voted Daniel Ortega, the Head of the then Junta, back as their President. He's now president of Nicaragua and good friends with President Maduro of Venezuela, who is considered a dictator and responsible for the socioeconomic decline of his country.

It was an interesting time and everyone kept saying, 'We're living history, we're living history." By the eighth year, I was sick of living history. We were going to be in Nicaragua for only two years. We ended up staying ten years.

In 1991, when Ian was on the verge of retirement, we came to Portugal. We had some great friends here that we'd met in Nicaragua. He was the Charge d'Affaires of the Swedish Embassy. We visited them a couple of times, noting that their children were at the international school outside Lisbon. We also wanted an international education for our boys, but not boarding school in the U.K., so we decided on Portugal. Another Portuguese friend in Nicaragua, whose husband worked for one of the aid organizations, had an attic in Lisbon, near the Palacio de Belem, that we rented when we first arrived. Each morning we'd catch the train to get the boys to school.

The house we eventually bought was the first house we looked at. And now that Ian was retired, we agreed that it was my turn to work. The role of Admission's Officer opened up at the boys' school. I applied, got the job, and worked there for almost 20 years, until long after the boys had graduated. I retired in 2012.

The boys grew up in Nicaragua, they spent their adolescence in Portugal and now they both live in the U.K. I feel as though they've completed the circle: my father started in the U.K. before launching a life in Latin America and the boys were born in Latin America and now they've launched their lives in the U.K.

I feel Brazilian. That's where I was born and grew up. When I go to England I don't feel English, even though I sound British. I was educated in British-style schools, but I'm not from a particular place in the U.K. so I don't feel I belong there. I interact with English people more here in Portugal than I do when in England where I find the English to be very insular. Probably if I went back to Brazil I would have a similar experience. I've been away so long that I don't belong there either. I've become a mishmash of cultures!

I've lived in Portugal 24 years now and that's the longest I've lived anywhere! It's Old Europe here. It's certainly not like Brazil. The European Portuguese are far more reserved. I have maybe two Portuguese friends, despite the fact that I speak the language fluently. The internationals I meet are fun and open. I can always find someone to relate to or who understands me, whereas if we internationals went back to the countries where we're from ... actually, I don't believe in going back. I just know that in England I don't belong, however I love visiting my sons and my granddaughter.

Where is she now?

Penny had a health scare a couple of years ago. She took time out from hiking and her various social activities, such as her weekly bridge games, to heal and restore. I bumped into her a few times when she was on the road to recovery, gently walking with a friend on the paredão between Estoril and Cascais, still wearing a splash of red and determined that she'd be back hiking in no time. These days she is hiking again and thoroughly enjoying her retirement, while also eking out time to visit her sons and her young granddaughter in the U.K.

Camilla Norrfjell

Introducing Camilla

James A Michener's 1971 novel *The Drifters* features six, 20-somethings traveling through Spain and Portugal and parts of Africa during the 1960s. One of these characters is a beautiful blonde and tanned Norwegian girl named Britta. When Camilla talked of her "bumming around" years, I thought of her as a Swedish version of Britta, but I admit, only for the most obvious reasons: they were both blonde Nordic females, they'd both traveled in the same areas of Europe, and at around the same time. In truth, I found it exciting and just a bit glamorous to hear from someone whose twenties had mirrored the character from a book that I'd really enjoyed reading as a teen. More intriguing, however, is the fact that Camilla's life, travels, adventures, and the people she encountered along the way are not from the pages of a best-selling Michener novel – they are real!

In her words

When I was 5, my young sister Anika, drowned. The nanny was on the phone and Anika got out of her playpen, ran down to the lake and drowned in 50 cm of water. I was sent to live with my grandmother for a while, but I remember little about this other than my parents forbidding my brother and me to talk about Anika. I don't know how my parents got over the loss, but I do know that my father took care of Anika's grave until he died in 2010.

We left Sweden and Udaholten, a tiny town in the middle of the country where I was born, when I was 12. My father was working for a steel company and he was promoted to head up the Brazilian office in São Paolo, where in the mid 1950s Sweden was exporting a lot of manufacturing. Father went ahead in 1953 and my mother, brother and I joined him in 1955. We traveled by boat with all our household effects. I thought once we arrived that I'd like to have a monkey as a pet – that was the extent of my understanding of where I was going to live!

The Brazilian economy was thriving at that time and expat Swedes employed by big companies sent their kids to international schools, and traveled back to Sweden every two years. We also had a driver and a cook. My brother and I went to a parochial school, St. Paul's, with other kids from all over the world, including countries in political turmoil such as Hungary, which in 1956 was in the midst of the "Hungarian Uprising," and Egypt which in 1956 was suffering under the impact of the Suez Canal crisis.

English was the main language at St. Paul's. I'd already had classes in English in Sweden and was proficient. Latin, French and remedial Portuguese were also on offer. I had Portuguese-speaking Brazilian friends in the neighborhood where we lived, so I quickly picked up Brazilian Portuguese. I also had a friend, Jacqueline, whose mother was my French teacher at St. Paul's. We had a weekly lunch together, which encouraged me to improve my spoken French. One of my father's business partners had three children, one of whom was my first friend in Brazil. Sylvia left Brazil with her family for Germany and in 1972 she was one of the guides at the Olympic games in Munich where she met the Swedish prince, who later became her husband. She went on to become Queen Sylvia of Sweden, married to King Carl XVI Gusta.

Prior to this, Sylvia continued to visit Brazil with her family and I saw her during her visits, but over time, we lost contact. As it turned out, when I first met Sylvia, the future Queen of Sweden, she had a pet monkey. It had got into her mother's creams and makeup and made a terrible mess in the bedroom and all over the mirrors. I realized that I would probably never have a monkey as a pet.

My father wanted me to go to a posh Swedish boarding school; he'd already made a reservation for me to attend. Before I was due to go, he rented a room for me in Paris so I could brush up on my French. It was the summer of 1960 and I spent it at the Sorbonne learning about French culture and history. I also went to Allianz Francais to improve my French grammar. Father was a Francophile. He had been responsible for the Swedish Chamber of Commerce in Marseille in 1934, before he married my mother. He and my mother would speak French when we were kids so that we wouldn't know what they were talking about, though with my proficiency with languages, I began to pick up French listening to my parents speak it.

I was supposed to start at the posh boarding school in Sweden, after the Sorbonne summer semester, to prepare for university. I was 17. But there had been some sort of mistake and there was no place for me, which I was thrilled about! I prepared to go back to Brazil, but my father said, "You don't speak German, so you're going to Germany."

At this point, I spoke four languages: Swedish, English, French, and Brazilian Portuguese. German would be my fifth.

I'd had a summer in Vienna previously, where I'd begun to learn some German. I stayed with a family whose daughters were highly cultured. They loved opera. I came from the pop-music culture of Brazil. The clash of old and new world cultures was extreme. I didn't want to go to Germany so my father suggested a Swiss boarding school. I didn't want to do that either. We agreed on a finishing school owned by Germans, but in Austria, in a mountainous area where the focus was on the outdoors, skiing, sailing, learning German, cooking, and mother-care classes.

Thirty girls from all over the world attended the school. My capacity with language resulted in me doing much of the translation for the other girls. I had a foot in many different cultures and countries and my first memory of adapting to this was at that finishing school. I went with Ursula, one of my friends, to her house outside Munich, and there I discovered that the rituals of Christmas were different than in Sweden. Ursula's family didn't wrap their presents; instead, each person had a little table with their unwrapped gifts on the table. This gave me an appreciation for cultural differences.

After finishing school I went back to Brazil and did equivalent exams. I wanted to study languages. I chose Geneva University as my father encouraged me to leave Brazil. I believe he was concerned that I'd marry a Brazilian, which he didn't want for me, fearing that I'd lose my freedom. My application was accepted, but ironically students were required to choose their mother tongue as their main language. The problem was that Swedish was no longer my best language. I switched over to economics.

I didn't finish my degree as I was diagnosed with Lupus and it had progressed to the point where I could barely button my clothes and do daily routines. With the Lupus under control on daily doses of cortisone, I went to London where I worked as a secretary. From London I drove back to Geneva. And in the summer of 1965, I drove down to Palma Mallorca in my old Volkswagen. I rented a house and worked in a hotel as a translator. A friend came with me, and while I worked hard at the hotel, my gorgeous, blue-eyed friend, Margaret, from Stockholm, met lots of boys at the beach and had quite a social life.

It was a good summer for me too – I've never been as thin as I was then! I had an Arab boyfriend and friends from all over the world, rich friends and some not rich, and I spoke their languages. The biggest challenge was the Lupus, and traveling with my first dog, a dachshund that needed shots and papers to cross borders. At the end of that summer I went back to Geneva. I had a job with an American company located in France that was building villas in Torremolinos, Spain. I was doing admin work for them and I ended up staying almost three years.

At some point during those few years I met the film actor Stewart Granger at a party. We were really into each other. Maybe he was into me as I was less than half his age, blonde and Swedish, and I was into him because he was gorgeous. Anyway, we ended up spending a night together. In the early 1970s I went back to Brazil by boat. I met a beautiful Argentine man, a model named Oscar. We were sharing cabins with other people. We couldn't do anything unless the cabin was empty, which was at lunchtime. So we didn't eat! But he didn't have any money and he kept asking me for money. I ended up giving him about 1,000 dollars. I got off the ship at São Paulo and he continued to Buenos Aires. He said he'd pay me back and that he loved me, but, of course, *nada*.

In 1973, I went to New York with a big multi-national company that I worked for. They were training me in advertising. I stayed in New York a year and a half and then went back to Brazil and worked for a couple more agencies, like Ian Rubican. During the next eight-to-ten year period, I worked my way up in advertising, working with two or three different agencies, sometimes a sidestep, sometimes stepping up. I had a nice apartment and life was good.

But then something happened toward the end of that period and it was the last straw.

I went to the cinema with a friend, parking the car opposite the cinema and we went in, but the film wasn't playing so we went back to the car and as we were getting into the car a boy approached us. He asked for money, saying he'd taken care of our car while we were away. But my friend, who is as feisty as me, said to the boy, "We were only gone five minutes sorry, no money."

We got into the car and were looking at the newspaper for another movie option. I looked in the rear view mirror and I saw this boy coming at the car with a baseball bat, readying to smash the car windows. I managed to put the car in first gear and take off, all the while thinking, "I'm 43, is this the way it's going to be now? When I'm a little old lady in São Paulo is this what it's going to be like, too unsafe to go out?"

In 1985 I realized I needed to leave Brazil. I wanted to feel safe and I longed to go somewhere where there'd be four seasons. Brazil doesn't have seasons! I was drawn to Europe. I felt more European than Brazilian. A Portuguese man I was involved with, who I'd met in Brazil and who I'd spent a summer with in Portugal, had introduced me to his country and I loved it. So I reasoned, "Why not Portugal?" I could speak the language and the market for advertising professionals was good – there wasn't a lot of competition back in the mid-1980s.

My decision to move to Portugal had nothing to do with the relationship with my Portuguese boyfriend. I knew it wouldn't last; he wanted me to be more mysterious and seductive. *Me!* Mysterious! I went ahead and sold my apartment in São Paulo to my neighbor, and I came to Lisbon in 1986 and rented an apartment in Lapa, a neighborhood in Lisbon. Not long after, I found work with an ad agency in Lisbon.

When I think about it, the cinema incident was a big turning point in my life. I'll never forget it. It was the reason I moved to Portugal.

I'm lucky, things have always worked out for me. Some would think I'm not so lucky as there was no big love in my life and I never married. I don't lament this; I think I wouldn't have managed. I feel as though there are certain flaws in my character that would have made a close relationship very difficult.

Nor did I have children. As a result of the Lupus, I had growths on my ovaries and fallopian tubes, which I subsequently had removed. I never felt motherly, and I certainly was not going to put my life at risk to have children. If I was to make a choice between children and dogs, which I guess I did, it's dogs for me! The Lupus is in remission now, but it's a chronic disease. In my 20s I was taking a lot of cortisone and immune suppressors. Now I only take five grams of cortisone every other day.

I'm very comfortable in my own company but periodically I feel lonely. To counteract this I have an active and social life. I take Italian language and pilates classes. I enjoy the Sintra Walks, and I still run my own home-based small business through which I have regular contact with clients. I enjoy being at home with my dog, Zen, a rescued hunting dog and a sweet little mutt. I also like to travel still, but not on my own. I prefer the company of a friend so that the trip becomes more about spending time with them.

One of my friends recently suggested that we go to Greece. I said, "I don't speak Greek, let's go somewhere where I speak the language!" I speak English, Portuguese, French, and Swedish fluently, and I have some fluency in Spanish, German, Italian, Norwegian and Danish. Another friend was planning a trip a year in advance. She wanted me to consider coming with her, but I refused. I don't plan that far ahead. I'm organized, but I'm not a planner like that, but I am planning on staying here in Portugal.

Where is she now?
Camilla is still enjoying her home and life in Portugal, just as she describes it. Her dear old "mutt" Zen is feeling his

age; consequently they participate less frequently on the Friday Sintra Walks. Instead, Camilla has turned her guest room into an art studio so she can paint and invite friends over to paint with her.

Sarah Eckt

Introducing Sarah

Sarah was vigorously massaging the back of her neck when we first met at a lunch in Cascais. I noticed that, her intensity, and how wound up she was. When I found out she'd not long returned from Myanmar with her work as a Human Rights Lawyer specializing in child protection, I was not at all surprised by how stressed she appeared. I have an enormous amount of respect and admiration for the work that Sarah does, given the current state of our chaotic world where children are too often victims. It takes a special individual to handle the emotionally tough cases that she's confronted with in her area of expertise. Just hearing about some of what she comes up against causes me to tear up. I was heartened to hear that she's found Lisbon a soft place to land, the perfect place to retreat, relax, and unwind.

In her words

My maternal grandmother was one of 11 children. She and her twin brother escaped Nazi Poland in the late 1930s, fleeing to Australia where she went on to marry and have six children. My mother was the second youngest and when she was 8, her father died. My grandmother, with no skills, was left to raise the children on her own, although her twin brother was around. I don't know much about my grandmother's other siblings and the wider family. Some survived the Holocaust; many did not.

My paternal grandfather, who was from Budapest, Hungary, survived the war. He was a book publisher and an intellectual. My father was born in 1947 and when he was 14, the story goes that a black car arrived and took my grandfather away. He was never seen again. So that, coupled with my father growing up under communism, actually it was fascism, was also traumatic. My father escaped Hungary when he was 18, smuggling himself across the border into the former Yugoslavia where he took a ship to Italy and sought political asylum. He sought refugee status in three countries – Canada, the U.S.A. and Sweden – and ended up in Sweden.

My parents met when they were traveling. In those days, one of the only acceptable places for a young Jewish woman to travel on her own was Israel, and that's where my parents met. My mother was desperate to strike out on her own, and she saw marriage as a way to do that. My parents subsequently married in Australia and then went back to live in Sweden, which is where my twin brothers and I were born.

When I was three and half years old, one of the twins died in infancy from cot death. My mother wanted my brother to be buried near her father, and for her, where you bury your child is where you spend the rest of your life. She also had this idea of being supported emotionally by her family, which was probably a bit misguided as they were never close. Anyway, those were the reasons for my parents relocating to Australia, which is how I came to grow up in Melbourne with my surviving younger brother. A third brother came along six years later.

When we arrived in Australia I was 5 years old and I only spoke Swedish. My parents enrolled me in a Yiddish-speaking primary school. I was simultaneously learning Yiddish and English, and so juggling three languages. I won an academic scholarship to a prestigious secondary school where it was compulsory to study a language. We had the choice of Bahasa (Indonesian), French, and Japanese, and I chose Japanese. I also did a student exchange to Japan. The Japanese girl came and stayed with us in Melbourne, and then I stayed with her and her family in Japan for a month.

At University, I did three study abroad programs: three months in the Netherlands, a year in Sweden (I wanted to go back to the country of my birth, but once there, attempts to recover "happier times" were elusive as I couldn't connect with my memories), and a six-month research placement in a Swedish-speaking area of Finland. All three of the programs were at Human Rights institutes. As a child, I loved the TV show *Perry Mason*, a criminal defense attorney who wins all his cases by proving his clients falsely accused. That program led me to believe that one of the ways to right the wrongs in the world was to become a lawyer, using the tools of justice. In both my studies and career, my area of focus was Human Rights.

My home life had been emotionally and physically violent as both my parents suffered intergenerational trauma as a result of the war and the Holocaust. My sense is that the unresolved tragedies of their past led to the highly dysfunctional and abusive environment in which I grew up.

Just as I was leaving the Netherlands for Sweden, my mother emailed a somewhat obscure email saying, "You must be in Sweden now. Make sure you have a warm coat, and I love you and I wish things had turned out differently." I didn't reply to the email immediately, as I was traveling the next day. When I arrived in Sweden I went to an Internet café and there was an email from my father saying that my mother had committed suicide. I was 23. Now, almost 18 years later, I still live with thoughts of "if only I'd replied to her email."

By my third year at university, I had this vision that I wanted to build schools for children. I'd had teachers who believed in me and supported me. I'd thrown myself into my studies, and into social justice campaigns – the reading, the study and the subsequent straight A's – education was my savior and my escape, and it's what got me through the dysfunction of my family and home life. My thinking was that that's what I could help facilitate for other children.

My life experiences, visions of a better world for children, and my studies coalesced when I graduated with a double degree with honors, followed by a Master's in International Development and a Ph.D. in Human Rights Law, all of which lead to a career in Child Protection in Emergencies.

In 2004 through 2005 I was in Timor-Leste. A colleague and I set up a Non-Governmental Organization (NGO) to do psychosocial support for children focusing on human rights for children, non-violent discipline and non-violent conflict resolution. We worked with children, parents, teachers, police, and with youths in prison. While in Timor-Leste, I also did an internship with the U.N. criminal tribunal, a hybrid national / international Human Rights Tribunal that had been created specifically to hear cases against Indonesian military, police, and Timorese militia involved in the post-referendum violence of 1999.

In 2007, I went to the U.S. to do some research. I met the man who eventually became my husband. He was a photographer who had worked in Nepal doing literacy through photography – he'd worked with children using photography as a means for self-understanding and self-expression. We moved back to Australia together and eventually bought a lovely little home in a beautiful rural town, but my work started to take me abroad so much that I was more often away from Australia than there.

In 2011, two weeks after we moved into our new home, I went to Darfur to work for an NGO. There I spent a year and a half doing child protection work with communities, and children who had been displaced by the Janjaweed militia. It was a bleak experience. Darfur was a desert of concrete, sand, and barren trees. We were a team of three men and three women working together and we used to joke about rubbish bag trees: tree branches encased with plastic bags that had blown about in the desert and become tangled in the bare tree branches. My heart just ached for green and for the sight of water. The accommodation was a brick hut with a generator and the toilet was a pit latrine in a corrugated iron shack. Locally available food was limited in range and quality.

My time in Timor had been much easier. There was a sense of life there. It was green and lush and there were supermarkets and cafes. We'd drink fresh coconut water after work and I'd go running on the beach and then go swimming. Darfur was tough. It had nothing. Life was a routine of home to the office, back home for lunch, back to the office, and then back home again for dinner and that's it.

Every three months I'd have R&R and fly back to Australia from Darfur. My husband couldn't come to Darfur to visit me as it was an off-limits region and I was there on a special visa authorizing me to work. The environment was highly, highly controlled. I was confined to one city and possibly my husband could have traveled to Khartoum, the capital, but there's no way he could have traveled to Darfur.

In 2012, after my stint in Darfur, I was offered a job in Guinea-Bissau, on the west coast of Africa, with the human rights section of the U.N. mission. It was a political stabilization mission and it meant moving out of child protection into human rights more generally. I chose it because it was a family duty station, which meant my husband could come and live with me, though my marriage was disintegrating by this point.

My focus in Guinea-Bissau was combatting impunity for political crimes and addressing human rights violations against women and children, in particular female genital mutilation, rape, and child early forced marriage. While in Guinea-Bissau, I met a 14-year-old orphan girl selling fruit on the streets. I helped get her back into school, and actually, I ended up adopting her. The adoption was finalized by the time she turned 16.

By 2015, my marriage was well and truly over and I expected I'd be on my own for some time, but then I met someone, a beautiful and unexpected surprise. He is Portuguese and he was also working in Bissau, for a development organization. By that stage I was starting to feel as though my work was no longer having an impact. There was also internal friction in my department and

I wasn't happy with the management. I decided it was time for me to move on from Bissau.

A job offer came through in Myanmar. It was not a secure position, and I could have stayed in Guinea-Bissau indefinitely since it was a fixed contract and a good salary, but I decided to take the temporary appointment in Myanmar. This position was with UNICEF and back in child protection. It was 2015 and Myanmar was an exciting country to be in as 50 years of military rule had just come to an end. Plus, it was another one of the three countries – Timor-Leste, Burma (now Myanmar) and Tibet – for which I'd done social justice campaigning in my early 20s, so I was excited at the opportunity to be working there.

I took the job and my partner and I embarked on a long-distance relationship. We agreed on this arrangement for a maximum of a year, after which he'd come and join me in Myanmar. But things went awry with his contract and he couldn't leave his position for 18 months. We decided we could cope with 18 months apart. Every R&R I had, we managed to rendezvous in Lisbon where we have an apartment, and where my adopted daughter is now living with my partner's mother, who is like a grandmother to her.

Almost a year into the Myanmar contract, my 40th birthday was fast approaching and I realized I was missing Australia and my connections there. So rather than R&R in Lisbon, I went back to Australia and gifted myself a "mindfulness retreat." On that retreat I stopped. Totally stopped. I became aware of just how exhausted and close to burn out I was. I hadn't processed things from my previous assignments; instead I'd just gone from one intense, emergency duty station to another, and then to another. And in Myanmar the intensity continued. It's now public knowledge, due to media reports, that up north the military were going through villages razing them, killing men, women and children, and raping women and girls. In retrospect, the work was causing me to feel traumatized on a near daily basis.

After the mindfulness retreat, I had a few coping strategies up my sleeve to help me self-soothe during times of stress. I also determined that I would do one more year and then take a break. Out of the blue, I received a call from Human Resources telling me that a decision had been made to "convert my post" which meant that the position no longer existed and that my contract would not be renewed. It was a huge shock! My 12-month plan went out the window, and along with it, my financial plan.

But the universe foisted upon me a break, which I may not have taken, if left to my own devices, since I'm sure I would have just applied for another post in another country and continued to push myself.

Since December 2016, I've been living in Lisbon taking extended R&R. I'm attending Portuguese language and culture classes several times a week, getting to know the country and city of my partner while learning his language. I'm also deepening my relationship with his mother, making new friends, taking care of myself and loving my life here. My identity and purpose in life was intimately tied to my work, so initially I felt lost. And I'd been so used to operating in a constant state of stress and distress that my nervous system was shot. I now have support professionals that I see regularly in Lisbon, and I'm feeling the difference.

What kind of work I'll do in the future and where, and whether it's contract work or consultancy where I do three months on and three months off, I'm not sure. My partner and I are also still figuring out how we can manage things so that we're living and doing fulfilling work in the same country. For now, it's about being in Lisbon and enjoying the fact that I'm more relaxed and much happier within myself.

Where is she now?

Two years on from this interview Sarah rubs the back of her neck a lot less. She is still based in Lisbon and now working independently from her home office with a child protection consultancy group of which she is a senior partner. Her partner is finalizing his work in Guinea-Bissau and thus their relationship is still long distance, though they steal precious time together in Lisbon, and abroad, when they have rare holidays together.

Tody Cezar

Introducing Tody

I participated in a restoration workshop that Tody offered through IWP and quickly learned that she's a stellar instructor of her highly specialized craft, and that she also swears like a trooper. Restoring valued objects to their former glory is fiddly, sometimes excruciatingly detailed work necessitating the emission of a few expletives here and there to release the tension of it all or so I found when trying to piece together the shattered edge of my beautiful Moroccan platter. I also discovered Tody is a very generous teacher, encouraging to the degree that I actually believed my skill in her workshop could be applied to a second career in restoration! And then not long after, I discovered something else: it turns out "Tody" is a family nickname. Her given name, Mildred, was the name of the housekeeper who came to the family after working for the great American playwright, Eugene O'Neil, and apparently Tody's mother was very fond of Mildred.

In her words

When I was young, my parents traveled a lot and my siblings and I would go to kid's camp. When my parents lost all their money, they didn't travel again until we were grown. As a young adult, I met them in Ireland once, and I went to Baja California with my father, and to Jamaica – my mom was Jamaican, though her forebears were originally from Portugal.

My aunty, who still lives in Jamaica, traced the family genealogy. Apparently our descendants left during the Inquisition and eventually found their way to Jamaica. First they went to Amsterdam, and then to Curaçao, and finally Jamaica. Long before Jamaica was British it was a Spanish island; given that the Spanish language was similar to Portuguese, perhaps that's the reason they settled there.

After my mother's father left Jamaica, he rented his house to some cousins. There were some kids from my family playing and someone said, "Oh that's a painting of our grandfather," and some black kids said, "He's our grandfather too."

When my mother visited Portugal, I remember her commenting that when walking the streets, "It was like seeing the whole family." And now when I look out the window I too see all my aunties in the faces of the Portuguese women.

My father's family is from the Ukraine. He and my mother met in New York, where he was renting an apartment from some Jamaicans and she was going to art school. I was born in the city. We moved when I was 4 and when my mother was pregnant with her fourth child. I think my parents decided it was time to get out of an apartment so they bought a house in rural New Jersey. I grew up there, but I always wanted to be someplace else.

My father's family were Russian Jews who struggled just to survive. I went to Odessa in the Ukraine, but there are no records. My grandmother had lost touch with our Odessa relatives. During WWII there was mass killing, so if the Nazis hadn't killed them Stalin might have. I did go to a graveyard, but there were no names. My grandmother would never talk about it, whereas my mother's family came with colorful stories and from a position of privilege – not money, but privilege. I certainly feel closer to my mom's side. They're so mad, funny, and totally outrageous.

When I was young I was quite shy and not sure of myself and I wasn't very good in school, and everybody would say, "Oh you can't do this and you can't do that," but I did anyway.

I married at 19 so I could go to Europe with my boyfriend. In 1963 you wouldn't just go off traveling with your boyfriend! But it turned out he was gay so that marriage lasted about 10 minutes. We got as far as Switzerland. I came home and finished school, and started my Master's in Art Education. By that time I was involved with a musician. He was in music school in Boston and he and I lived together. Unfortunately, it was only good half the time, so we split up.

While in Boston, my father died (my mother had died earlier). I went back to New Jersey to prepare the enormous family house for sale. It took about a year and a half of hard work and when it did sell, my sister and I split the money.

I'd had a small business making ceramic jewelry that I tried to resurrect after the house sale, but my heart wasn't in it anymore. Since the 1966 Florence floods, I'd always been interested in art conservation. I looked into studying conservation and discovered that you need chemistry and algebra. Despite not being a good student, I thought this is the time to do it. I ended up studying Art Restoration in England and once I moved there, I knew I wasn't going back to the U.S.

Given my Jamaican heritage, I thought I'd be able to stay in England. I was wrong. When I finished school, I had six months before I needed to leave. At my school's Halls of Residence, I'd met a Portuguese woman and I ended up visiting her. Later, she wrote me that there was a job here – a huge mirror needed gilding. I took the job.

I rented out my flat in the U.K., packed my bags and arrived in Lisbon on a Sunday, and started work on Monday. This was 1998. I stayed with that company for a year, but I was so unhappy. I called my aunt in Jamaica, and I said, "I can't do this anymore" and she said, "Come home." I wasn't really legal in Portugal, so I flew to England and then I caught a plane to Jamaica.

In time, I was ready to come back, but I never really worked in Portugal again. It's difficult here; there's not the same kind of equity that you might have in the U.K., the U.S. or Australia. I found out much later that I was the most highly trained person on a staff of 26 people but the lowest paid. I felt really taken advantage of. If I'm really honest, probably I was part of the problem; I'd finished all this training and I was a bit arrogant.

I didn't want to go back to the States and I couldn't go back to England so I stayed in Portugal. I started looking for work on the *Conservation/Restoration* website where I saw something in Kosovo. I made enquiries and they asked me to do an inspection for the U.N. of damage to churches and Mosques. I'd completed an internship at the British Museum so I went back to their library to research, but there wasn't much about Kosovo or Balkan art. I knew Kosovo had had a war, but that was about all I knew!

The plane was supposed to land in Macedonia, but there was fog so we landed in Sophia, Bulgaria and when I disembarked it was like a scene from an old black and white movie. By the time the bus arrived at the border of Macedonia, where someone from Kosovo was supposed to be waiting for me on the other side, it was much later than the original plan. I must have looked lost because a man, not my Kosovo connection, asked if I needed a ride, he said he could take me to Pristina. We ended up driving most of the night and eventually I arrived at my hotel.

On the job inspecting these monuments, I met a local man, who eventually became my lover. He actually knew what he was doing, thank God, as I didn't! He was treated rather badly by the U.N. people. I remember once he got up to speak as the expert, and they said, "Sit down, we have our expert here," referring to me. And I said, "You have an expert, but it's not me, it's this man." Local people weren't given consideration at all.

After the work with the U.N., I was asked back to work in a Mosque that had been damaged. I didn't know anything about Islamic art, but I discovered that in the Balkans it's so colorful! We worked on and off in that Mosque for nine years. It was really challenging and incredibly rewarding. There was a lot to be done. They built a new minaret as it had been destroyed. The door was badly damaged as there'd been attempts to burn the whole building. I restored the door. I'm very proud of that. It was such a beautiful thing. There were panels that needed to be completely replaced. The charred panels had been saved so I'd have some idea of what had been there. There was enough information so that I could work from those panels.

Getting the resources we needed in Kosovo was difficult. When I was asked to do the interior wood panels, I said, "Great." I submitted my shopping list, stressing the need for *alcohol* and *acetone,* saying it absolutely needed to be there for me to do the work. When I arrived, I went through our supplies: there was some alcohol, some cotton wool, and no acetone, though I found five little jars of nail polish remover. WTF!

I called the project manager and I said to him, "I find it alarming that you don't know the difference between a liter and a milliliter and that you don't know the difference between nail polish remover and acetone, but not to worry, my team is out on the lawn doing their nails!"

UNESCO was on our back, "When is it going to be done, when is it going to be done?" I said, "It'll be done as soon as you get me the varnish." This would happen day after day after day. At some point, I just let loose, "Get me the f'ing varnish and then it'll be done!" Oh God, it could be so frustrating.

After I came home from my first trip to Kosovo, I unpacked my winter clothes and went to India for two months to work outside Chennai in a museum. When I returned, I went back to Kosovo. The next year, 2002, they didn't have the funds for us to do any further work. I ended up going to China to teach English for a year instead.

I had an online interview with this guy and he asked me, "How do you spell color?" And I said, "When I spell it for you, I spell it c-o-l-o-u-r." And he said, "Oh very good." And he kept giving me words, and I kept saying, "Well when I'd spell it for you, I'd spell it ..." And he said, "You spell very well for an American!" No shit! Everyone thinks Americans are painfully stupid.

Teaching English was not my cup of tea. I enjoy teaching workshops on restoration. That's something I'm passionate about. While in Beijing, I knew I couldn't go a year without doing something that I love so I volunteered at Peking University in their conservation lab for the time I was there. I made great friends.

The conservation community around the world is small and competitive, which may be the reason that it's also amazingly hostile. It's such a shame as basically what we're about is fixing things and making them look nice. I was asked back to restore the painted wood inside the Mosque in Kosovo and when I arrived I thought we're going to do this differently. I'd got to the point where unless I'm in charge, I wouldn't do it. At least if I'm in charge I can set the tone and there's no nastiness on the job.

I also worked a lot in England. I'd hear through the grapevine about jobs that were available. A friend of mine owns a restoration company that does a lot of work for the big English auction houses, and I would work with this company whenever they needed help. Through a former tutor, I landed a job working on the Crown Bar glass in Belfast. It's a Victorian High Gothic bar that's a famous tourist attraction due to its beauty and the fact that it's still standing after so many terrorist bombings. I had the best time working on that.

At some point I went back to China, to Yushu, an area near the border of China and Tibet. To get to Yushu, I took a 32-hour sleeper bus, with no toilets or food stops, to a remote area at altitude. I didn't realize how remote it was. The temple there had been destroyed in a massive earthquake. The work was interesting as the temple walls were all mud and I'd never worked on something like that before.

The following year, I went to Sikkim, which is in the foothills of the Himalayas. I worked with a French woman with whom I'd previously worked; this time she was not very nice. I thought, 'I don't need this!' I mean, this one was not talking to that one, and that one was not talking to this one! All so bloody stupid, so I left.

It was the beginning of August and I realized I could completely circumambulate India. I started at the point on the border of China and Tibet and ended up in Chennai. I'd worked in the museum there before and I wanted to say hello to friends. It was many days on trains and buses and it was quite a rough trip and I got quite ill. As I was coming back to Chennai I got a call asking if I'd work in a museum I'd worked in 12 years before. I said, "Yep."

I have a good friend who works at the British Museum, where there's a lot of support and resources, which was something I wanted at one time. I'm glad I didn't go that route. Instead, I went to these incredible places where there's minimal-to-no resources, and you just have to make it work. You have to rely on local people and your team and just do what you do even if that means breaking some rules. In order to do the job as best you can in places where there are no resources, you do have to break some rules of the craft.

In Sikkim they use yak butter for their lamps, so everything gets very black. The woman I was working with said, "Tody, do you think you could get this black off?" And I said, "I don't know, what have you tried?" She was a traditionalist with all these formulas, and I was like, "You know what, I'm gonna try some soap." And I got a bar of soap and I cleaned the black off.

I was working at a new museum in London. We were cleaning marble fireplaces with metal backs, which were all rusty. We cleaned them off, but they still looked like crap. So I got some black shoe polish and white spirit and did them up and they looked great! My colleague was so anxious about this. I said, "If anyone asks, tell them you used black pigment and micro-crystalline wax." That's what shoe polish is.

I think of myself as retired now, though I do a lot of volunteer work, such as in India, where in return for my time, my expenses are paid. This works for me since it's so cheap to live there. India is a tough place to work, however, due to the inequality and the way people are treated. I try to do things differently in the effort to let people know that not everybody is going to take advantage of them. I do my best to "pay it forward" in countries that have been kind to me.

After the Kosovo war, people had lost touch with their heritage. They'd either lost skills or they hadn't had the chance to learn. Part of our job was to teach them how to care for their heritage. Lots of people in Kosovo hadn't even been in the Mosque! I would invite people in saying, "Come on in, this is yours." I'd always have an area for little kids, where they couldn't do any damage. I'd give them a scalpel and let them scrape away at something and I'd always take a picture and give it to them so they'd feel as though they were a part of the project. That kind of experience was often more important than the actual restoration work.

I've been on my own for a long time and I think that suits me. I went to Cape Verde recently with a woman whose partner has his place and she has hers. I like that arrangement, that'd work for me. They do a fair amount of travel together, but he doesn't like risky travel, so she calls me to do that. We went to Albania together, and Armenia, Azerbaijan and Georgia. When I go places I like meeting people – that's why I like working in countries like Kosovo and India, you get invited to weddings, circumcision parties, and all that good stuff.

I have an apartment here in Portugal, in a very working class area in Lisbon. I didn't want to live in a neighborhood with lots of expats. Where I live has given me the chance to develop some Portuguese friendships. All these years on, I still take Portuguese lessons. I can order my groceries at the local market, have basic conversations with my neighbors, and chat a bit with my Portuguese friends, that kind of thing.

When I'd been here about 12 years I met some women who were members of IWP. Up until then, I'd had such a hard time fitting in, but mixing with these women has given me the chance to talk to others in English and that has helped me feel less alone. I also have a flat in London but Portugal has always been the place I've come back to.

The way I feel about my life and my work is this: When things are easy it's like you're in a port and it's sunny; when you're out to sea, that's when you learn, when you're challenged. It's the hardest stuff that makes us grow. Thank God my work and travels really pushed me, otherwise I might have ended up a fat Jewish princess in bed eating bonbons!

Where is she now?

Tody explored getting Portuguese citizenship via the ratified Portuguese bill allowing descendants of exiled Sephardic Jews to apply for citizenship, but it was too complicated. In 2018, she ended up pursuing and was granted citizenship through mainstream channels. She then sold her flat in London and bought a beautifully restored apartment in the same neighborhood where she's been renting for years. She's planning on moving into her new home soon.

Joanne Tangye

Introducing Joanne

Jo and I shared a table at a workshop on restoring broken household items. Tody Cesar, an Art Restorer, who also appears in this book, gave the workshop. Joanne had a ceramic platter with a large chunk out of it and I did too. With heads down, hard at work, following Tody's instructions on piecing ceramics back together with no sign of a break, Jo and I shared a few stories, had a few laughs and agreed to rendezvous a couple of months later in Sydney, where we were both going to be for Christmas 2015. We met at the Sydney Botanical Gardens, and over cool drinks in the shade I learned that though Jo was born in Australia, she grew up in the isolated jungles of New Guinea, eventually raising a family in seven different countries.

In her words

When I was 3 months old we moved from Sydney, Australia to New Guinea (N.G.) where my parents set up house on a cocoa plantation about 20 miles from Rabaul on the island of New Britain. Our plantation was two miles from the nearest neighbor and about six miles from a very small primary school, an agricultural college, a golf club, and a general store. It was Land Rover and corrugated-dirt-road country and those roads washed away in the wet season. There were small villages in the jungle en route to Rabaul but we were pretty isolated on the plantation.

Our house was simple, open and airy, well suited to the tropical climate. We had a garden on 8 acres and the plantation beyond with a huge pineapple patch, papaya, guava, and pomelo fruit trees. There was space and freedom so we were outside all the time, climbing trees and racing around. We played with the local indigenous kids, the children of the men who worked on the plantation, and we mixed with the other expatriates.

The golf club was a point of social contact and in those days my parents had a very active social life and we kids were a part of that. At one stage, my parents had a station wagon and they used to put the backseat down and put a mattress in there and we would play and then sleep there until my parents were ready to drive home from the club. It was quite a life, a lot of fun actually.

One of my parents would drive us into school each day but for the last 18 months of my primary education, my mother home-schooled my younger brother and me, my two eldest sisters having already gone to boarding school. Mother loathed this set up and we loathed it too. As there were no secondary schools near us in N.G., at the age of 11 we all went to boarding school in Sydney. It was a huge culture shock, but it was a generational way of life for us. My father was born and grew up in N.G. and he and his siblings went to boarding school, traveling to-and-from by sea.

In the very early days we still took a boat to Sydney, but by 1964, I was flying to boarding school on a DC3 propeller-driven airplane with two rows of seats. We came home once a year at Christmas for about a month. During the other school holidays we stayed with my mother's aunt. Of all my siblings, I was probably the most homesick. I know it was difficult for my mother with her children so far away. We didn't have telephones on the plantation then. Mum would write to us every week, typing a letter with three sheets of carbon paper – four copies of the same letter – usually three typed pages, and she would handwrite one individualized page to each of us. Every week!

The absence of their children caused my parents to be very social and busy. It was the same for all the expat parents in N.G. My mother got a job running our general store, which also housed the post office. For many years, she ran both. I think without that work she would have gone crazy.

I wanted to be a teacher. I applied to a college that trained teachers to work in N.G., but they stopped taking Caucasian students the year I wanted to enroll. I had no backup plan. So at 19, I did a secretarial course in Sydney and I worked for the CSR, Australia's big sugar company, and I lived with my great aunt. Then my aunt died and though I thought I might take a flat in Sydney with one of my boarding school friends, that didn't work out. I went back up to N.G., where my father helped me get a job.

I settled into my new job and life back in N.G., and decided I wanted to travel. Suddenly I had some gumption! I also started to enjoy myself socially. There were people in N.G. from Australia, from other countries too, and everyone had traveled from somewhere else to get to N.G. and many were going on to different places.

We used to have a radio and we'd listen to the Australian Broadcasting Commission news and in those days the announcers sounded so terribly British. It was a bit of the outside world. Perhaps it was that, along with all the expats that made me curious about the world. We didn't have television back then so you couldn't actually *see* what the outside world looked like, apart from newspapers and magazines, like the National Geographic.

As well as my day job, I took a night job as a waitress, to save money to go overseas. It was in the restaurant where I met an Englishman, who ultimately introduced me to the man I eventually married. Richard had grown up on a farm in England and had also gone to boarding school. He'd already been to university and traveled independently in the late '60s – through Iraq and Iran and other Middle Eastern countries. After university he didn't want to go straight into a job, he wanted to do something else, so he joined an organization called Voluntary Service Overseas. Basically he said to them, "Send me as far away as you can," and they said, "How 'bout New Guinea?" and he said, "Where's that?"

Once we started to spend time together, it didn't take us long to decide that we'd travel together. I'd already begun to plan and save money, but in retrospect, I don't think I could have done it on my own. I still was very timid, though I did have big visions.

My first trip abroad was to the U.K. We flew separately to Sydney then met up, traveling overland by train, down to Melbourne, across to Adelaide, and over to Perth. From Perth, we sailed to Durban, South Africa, rented a car and drove the garden route to Cape Town, boarded the ship again, and sailed up the west coast of Africa and onto Rotterdam, disembarking in Southampton, U.K. From there we drove through the green English countryside, dotted with picture postcard villages. It was a revelation to me, this charming scene. I'd never seen anything like it!

I think my jaw dropped when we arrived at my future in-laws' home. Part of the house dates back to the 12th century, while the front is from the 1600s. Inside it was full of antiques, all very stylish and classy, and there was daily help in the kitchen, house, and garden. Now that was a culture shock!

My father had built the house I grew up in. It was wooden and on stilts, with lovely wooden floorboards and big windows, no electricity, no fancy furnishings, and with the kitchen and the bathroom inside. We called it the "New House". Our first house was more rustic: it was made of native materials and our sleeping and living quarters stood as separate buildings from the bathroom, which was separate from the kitchen.

We had help on the plantation and in the house too, but I still found Richard's parents' home and circumstances very intimidating. They still changed for dinner! The life they were living was not quite Downton Abbey, it was not that level of wealth, but it was quite formal and traditional. I don't know what they thought of me, this girl from the jungles of New Guinea, probably that I was terribly unsophisticated.

We married in the beautiful English gardens of my in-laws' home and a year later my husband received an offer to go to Montreal, to set up an office for the shipping company he was working for. We were there five years before the company moved us to New York for five years, where we had two children. The company moved us back to England for four years, where we had another two children.

After England we went to Singapore for 18 months, followed by Indonesia, Taiwan, and Hong Kong, living in those countries for about five years each. In Jakarta I did a 3-month training course to become a docent of Indonesia's Museum National, and for the next four years, I worked as a volunteer museum guide. While in Taiwan, I started a distance-learning program, earning my teaching certification, which opened the door for me to teach, which is what I'd wanted to do since my late teens. I was offered a job as a teachers' assistant at an international school in Taiwan, and also in Hong Kong, where I taught for another 2 years.

My children are third culture kids: born of parents from two different cultures, raised in a culture other than their parents'. In each of the places we lived the kids went to the local international schools. When they turned 13, we sent them to boarding school. We chose Sydney. It was in the same time zone as Asia, where we were living during the years the kids were in secondary school, and in Australia there were four school terms a year and we'd all see each other more often.

We also hoped that finishing up their secondary education in Australia would give them a sense of "place."

When my daughter had started high school in Hong Kong, she said she wanted to go to boarding school to be closer to her brothers. She missed them. At that point, I realized I didn't want to send another child away so I went to Australia and found a school that was both a day school and that took boarders, and I set up house in Sydney and I had all the children come and live with me. We hadn't lived together in such a long time. It was one of the best things I did.

It wasn't so easy for my husband, who stayed in Hong Kong where he was working, because for a while, we had a commuter marriage. The arrangement did help the kids get back to a sense of family, however, it was short-lived. The eldest went off to Russia for a year; the second went to Madagascar for three months and then Kenya for a year; the third one didn't move anywhere at that time. He preferred the stability of a permanent home in Sydney with some periodic travel. And the fourth one went off to Guatemala for five months, followed by Spain for a year.

During this period, my husband had been with a big Asian conglomerate. He'd spent 17 years in Asia working for them and he was given the option to retire at 57. The original idea was that he'd then come to Australia, since I was there with the kids, and find work. But an advertisement caught his eye for a position in England; he applied for it, and was shortlisted. We knew there were two other candidates, one of whom we felt would get the job, but blow-me-down, Richard got it! He accepted the offer and we moved to England. Our daughter, who was still at secondary school in Sydney, wanted to come too, which meant for years 11 and 12 she was going to be with us in England. We found her a school, and we all settled into our routines.

The organization my husband worked for required that he travel a great deal. Due to his absence, and some other factors pulling us back to Australia, my daughter and I stayed only six months in England, before returning to Sydney. The children were in their late teens and early 20s by this stage and they really needed a parent. All sorts of issues, problems and anxieties come up at that age. I understood this. I'd experienced this at their age so I wanted to be there for my children.

Fortunately, I managed to get a job in Sydney. I started in 2005 and stayed for 10 years. I worked in a large independent school as a Special Needs teacher with a little boy who had a visual impairment. In order to do my job well, I learned to read and type braille and while I enjoyed the work and the relationship I'd built with my student, the work became dry, black and white. I like color and getting messy with art and in that regard, I'm a much happier person teaching younger children. When I was working with this little boy, I applied to teach in the pre-school. To my delight, I was given the job.

After England, Richard was offered a job in Bangladesh, which he accepted. He makes these choices, and I allow it. It's what keeps him alive. Initially I went with him, but at the time, I felt I just couldn't move countries again, so I stayed in the job I enjoyed, and close to my friends and the life I'd built up in Sydney. Once again we embarked on a commuter marriage.

Eventually we lived together again for a couple of years in Sydney. I was working full-time while my husband did some consultancy. It was a valuable transition period because out of the blue an opportunity in Portugal came to us via someone Richard had met seven years earlier. The timing was right for us to move together to Lisbon. At that point the kids were in their late 20s and early 30s. They had their own lives and were settled.

We were excited about the adventure of living on mainland Europe, where we'd not lived before. Additionally, we saw this move as an independent choice, like our moves to Montreal and New York, and unlike our Asian posts where we were moved according to the needs of the company, which we accepted, because of the expatriate benefit package that comes with working for these multinational enterprises.

After a four-month journey involving a sea voyage from Southampton to New York and a train across Canada and back across the United States, we arrived in Lisbon late August 2015, the month my husband's new position commenced in Lisbon. Our trip went amazingly well; we got on the whole time, much to our surprise! Though we've done a lot of traveling, separately and together, we'd not traveled together for as long as four months at a stretch.

Portugal is a two-year contract. I've been here only six months and I'm aware that people are genuinely friendly and welcoming here. I don't recall this speed of settlement in past moves and I wonder if it is unique to Portugal or a mix of factors such as my stage of life, the climate, influence of outward-looking people, and the diversity of the women I've been meeting through IWP who have certainly contributed to the positive experiences I've had here.

I do see myself returning to spend our "winter years" in Australia. Though I doubt that Richard will ever stop working full time. There'll always be another offer for him, and he's a restless person. He cannot be still. My husband is extremely lucky to have me! And I'm lucky too as he has been the agent for movement in my life. In him, I found someone who wanted to be my travel partner.

All the kids have dual citizenship and they do see that due to our lifestyle they have a lot of choice. They've all returned to Sydney to live after some years in the U.K. and Belgium for two of them, while our second son lives in Washington D.C. with his Mexican wife, which is where their careers are based. Family life is never static though, as the stable third son is now considering a move overseas.

I'm actually a reluctant traveler, but I like being in foreign places. This may be the result of feeling we were foreigners in N.G., and then I also felt like a foreigner at boarding school. Perhaps it's because I know how to be a foreigner. The paradox is I do love this itinerant lifestyle, even though at times I have found it to be extremely difficult.

Where is she now?

As I write, it is the beginning of the 2018 school year and Joanne and Richard are still in Portugal. They both continue to travel a lot, Jo schedules visits to Australia to spend time with her adult children, and also to Washington D.C. where she loves her role as "granny nanny" to one of her grandchildren. And this past school year, Jo took a part-time teaching job at Richard's school and she also began tutoring some international students in English.

Rosemary Mellahn

Introducing Rosemary

I first met Rosemary on an IWP small bus tour. She sat next to me with earplugs in her ears, listening to classical music on her iPod. Immediately I noticed things about her, such as her glossy black hair pulled back over her ears into a ponytail. I had a sense that she was probably about my age, even though there was no trace of grey in her black mane. I wondered about her heritage. Her dark eyes and dark olive skin suggested southern European or perhaps Indian. After the first pit stop on the IWP tour, we settled back into our respective seats and now with her earplugs out, we talked. Very quickly she told me things that I found quite curious such as the unknown origins of her father, and the mysterious karmic pull that in her 20s had drawn her to Portugal, where she eventually decided she wanted to live. It was obvious to me that some sort of greater force was at play in her life, one that led me to conclude that she was living out the unlived life of her father.

In her words

I'm from a very conservative Afrikaans background and at age 22, I married. It was a mistake, we were too young, but South Africa (S.A.) was so conservative in 1979, Johann and I couldn't just live together. Unfortunately, we didn't know about life or how to behave as a couple. However, the relationship took my life in a direction that it might not have gone.

Six months after we married, Johann was transferred 1000 km across S.A. to East London, and I went with him. It was the first time that I'd traveled so far away from my parents, who lived in Cape Town where I was born. A year and a half later, Johann was transferred 300 km back in the direction of Cape Town – to Port Elizabeth. I realized I needed to learn how to adapt.

In Port Elizabeth I worked with civil engineers and my career in that area began, but six years after we married, we went back to Cape Town and at that point, I made the decision to leave Johann. The engineering company could transfer me to Pretoria, but I didn't want to go there either, it was too conservative. Instead, I asked a friend to drive the 1400 km from Cape Town to Johannesburg with me in my little VW Golf. I'd contacted another friend with a farm there and asked if I could come and stay for a while. Even though my money was running out, I felt positive. I was my own person again and I received a couple of job offers.

A year later in 1986, I came to Portugal. I had a South African-Portuguese friend named Liz. Her family lived in Mozambique, the former Portuguese colony, and I met her through my ex-husband's family. Liz was on her way to Germany and she suggested to me, and a mutual friend, Natalia, that we all meet in Lisbon. We stayed in Liz's parent's holiday apartment in Carcavelos, just outside Lisbon.

I recall sitting at Carcavelos train station in the sun and it must have been shining on my hair because Liz said to me, "You know you have Portuguese hair." She was pointing out that I could be Portuguese, but I didn't think twice. In S.A. there are a lot of people who have dark hair and olive skin.

Back then there was a popular disco in Cascais called *Coconut*, which is now the *The Hotel Farol*. One night we went to *Coconut* and I met Liz's cousin Rui. He was gorgeous! And the Latin music, it was so different from music in S.A.! We have an Afrikaans word *kuier* that means "to visit," but it can also mean "to socialize" or "to party" – this is the word I would use to describe the experience I was having in Portugal. It was *kuier*.

The next morning, we left for the north with Rui driving us in his small car. He didn't speak a word of English, but fortunately Liz spoke English and Portuguese. We drove to Mafra, to Óbidos, to Nazaré – there were no highways in those days. It was a very powerful experience for me visiting places like Óbidos, where I saw ruins from the 11th century. South African and Afrikaans culture seemed so young in comparison. We arrived in Nazaré very late at night and there was very little open except one restaurant that was about to close. Fortunately, they stayed open and cooked clams for us, that's all they had. We had a wonderful, rip-roaring time. I sat opposite Rui and that's when it really began. There was a connection between us. Rui was telling jokes and Liz was translating and we were screaming with laughter. We had such fun.

Within a short period of time, my impressions of Portugal were so very positive, which may well have been because Rui and I were falling in love.

Natalia and I decided that when Liz headed back to S.A., we'd backpack around Spain. I didn't want to leave Rui. I was in love with him, but due to the language barrier it was *muito complicado*! Even so, we ended up spending about ten days together. Liz went back to S.A. and I did go onto Spain with Natalia. I was so sad to leave Rui behind.

Natalia and I wanted to hitchhike along the Costa del Sol. In S.A. you would never hitchhike. It was too unsafe. We ended up back in Portugal in the Algarve and from there I came to Lisbon on my own so I could have a couple of days with Rui before returning to S.A. I don't know how we coordinated it all without a mobile phone or email, and without a common language, but when I got out of that bus in Lisbon, there was Rui, waiting for me. I spent two wonderful days with him and he showed me Sintra and Lisbon and then I went back to S.A. heartbroken. I never forgot him.

I see that some things are deep in our genetic code. My parents were born in Cape Town, and generally speaking, South Africans don't care where their forebears are from. But, once I came to Europe, people started questioning me about my background. As a result, I asked my mother and she traced three generations back and found Dutch and French Huguenots. That's where I get my really dark hair. I also look like my father, I have his dark eyes. He was half Portuguese and half Dutch. That's all we know as he was adopted.

My father knew one of his parents was Portuguese, but tragically, due to Apartheid, Afrikaners discriminated against all people with dark complexions. If my skin had been a bit darker, that would have been problematic. The Portuguese, the Chinese, the Japanese, the Greeks, they were not considered "white" by the Afrikaners.

My father was born in 1920 and the family that adopted him raised him as an Afrikaner. I think he was nationalistic and racist, but it was due to the way that he had been raised and the culture he grew up in. On top of that, he had an authoritarian personality. Deep down he was a kind person, but also very strict, and this was the norm for his generation in S.A. at that time. I grew up in an era where respect was very much a part of our education and my father demanded it, so I never took any of this up with him.

It wasn't until my father was 80 that I found out about his adoption. Prior to that time, including while I backpacked in Portugal, I had no clue that I was a quarter Portuguese. My mother told me that at 20, my father had had the opportunity to meet his birth mother, but he refused because it was shameful that his mother had become pregnant out of wedlock. He did not pursue finding his father either, presumably because he was Portuguese.

Unfortunately, his illegitimate birth gave him a chip on his shoulders. It was so scandalous, according to the Afrikaners' belief systems, which came from the harsh and extreme Calvinistic Dutch. It's a complex country and we have a lot of influences from strong peoples, the English, the Dutch, and the Germans. And, unfortunately, nothing could be traced of his adoption. I think the hospital probably noted, "child born out of wedlock." In 1920s South Africa, organizational and administrative functions were in many ways quite chaotic.

After that first visit to Europe, I went back to S.A. a changed person. I wanted to see more, travel more. I couldn't settle down. I was saving a lot of money working in Johannesburg and my friend Natalia, who I'd traveled with, also wanted to return to Europe and this time for a year. And then I met someone.

It was January 1987 and I was 29. I had a friend who moved onto a commune with people of different nationalities, and a guy living in this commune was my husband-to-be, a German with long blonde hair named Kai. Anthony, my friend, had been married to a Portuguese woman. When Kai met me for the first time on that January visit to the commune, he thought I was Anthony's ex-wife. He thought I was Portuguese.

Natalia and I agreed that we would travel back to Europe in March and the weekend before our departure, Anthony suggested we go camping. Even though I was not into camping, I agreed to go.

We drove up to Kruger National Park near the waterfalls. It was so beautiful! We stayed the weekend and when we drove back, we stopped off at the commune to have a coffee. As we were leaving, Kai walked in with an Irish girl and a German girl. They'd had a boozy lunch and perhaps that's why Kai said, "You can't leave now, we have to have a drink together." After that drink he asked me out even though I had told him I was leaving for Europe in two days.

He came to fetch me the following evening and we talked through until 4 a.m. The next evening we went out again, same thing, talk, talk, talk! On the third day, he took me to the airport and he had a bottle of French Champagne with him. We drank it at the airport and as I was getting ready to board, he gave me a letter suggesting I read it on the plane.

It was a very unromantic letter; just a "thank you" for three wonderful days and that I should promise to keep in touch. He was working for a German company. He said I could collect call anytime; his company would pick up the phone bill.

Natalia and I flew to Belgium first and we had a great time, backpacking through several countries. I did call Kai collect, and from then on, we were in constant contact.

When I started to run low on money, I went to London and worked as an au pair for a Greek Cypriot couple who had three kids and two successful restaurants in the West End of London. They were very rich and they appeared to have everything, everything except time for their three boys who were 10, 13 and 16. It was very sad and the experience of caring for these children whose parents were never around left a lasting impression on me. I decided that if I ever had my own children, I'd be different; I'd be there for them. I was the nanny for six months, but I kept in contact with those boys for 20 years.

Kai came to visit me in London, to tell me he was being transferred from Johannesburg to Hong Kong that November. And though Asia was not part of my travel plans, I told him that on my way back to S.A., I'd visit him in Hong Kong.

As December grew near, he let me know that he was going to spend Christmas with his parents in Hamburg, and would l like to come. I thought, "Oh God, what will they think, a divorced woman who is four years older than their son and a bit plump?" – I'd put on some weight while traveling. But they welcomed me with open arms and it was a wonderful experience, celebrating Christmas in cold northern Europe, after a lifetime of summer Christmas celebrations in the southern hemisphere. It was such a successful visit, Kai now really wanted me to come to Hong Kong and in fact, he booked a ticket for me.

After several weeks together in Hong Kong, we both knew we wanted to stay together. Eighteen months later we married and two years later my son was born but with great difficulty and thus I had just the one child. We lived in Hong Kong nearly seven years. It was a fascinating place, except when you have a child it's not so easy. In Hong Kong you work long hours. It's a city that's all about money and power. We would eat out a lot and entertain clients. This was the lifestyle.

When my son was around 3 it started to become stressful finding ways of occupying him constructively. We lived in an apartment and we needed to find places outside to go as a family. The problem was Hong Kong had very few parks and green spaces and then those spaces were always so busy and noisy with families and their children. Seven million people lived in Hong Kong then. Over time trying to eke out quality family time on the weekends turned stressful. We had a wonderful apartment with mountains at the back and in front a beautiful sea view, but you never heard a bird! There was a joke amongst the expats that the Chinese ate all the birds. They eat everything! Added to all this, Hong Kong was becoming too expensive for us, and so we went back to Hamburg to live.

Kai and I both love Germany, it's organized, everything works well, but we realized that once his parents were gone, we'd like to live somewhere else, somewhere warmer. We spent some time in Spain, where we had a second home in Denia, but we eventually sold it. It started to feel inauthentic and we got "Spained out."

However, the longer we lived in Hamburg the more entrenched we were in German culture. South Africa is sort of chaotic and disorganized, but I've always preferred things more structured and organized, like the Germans and I was aware I'd adopted German behaviors. As I got older people seemed unhappy to me, especially elderly Germans, which made me realize that I didn't want to end up looking or feeling like that. Hamburg is a place where 80 percent of the year it's a heavy grey, and certainly the weather can cause you to feel depressed and unhappy.

It's 28 years since I left S.A. When my son was born, I thought, "Even if this marriage doesn't work, I don't want to raise my son back in South Africa." I grew up hyperaware, always looking over my shoulder, concerned for my safety, and I wanted to protect my child from this.

We took a holiday in the Algarve, when our son was about 7, but it wasn't authentic Portugal. I remember saying to Kai, "One day, I'll show you the Portugal I experienced backpacking in the '80s." Sometime after that, Kai went to Lisbon for business and I went with him. After three days in Lisbon, we went to Cascais. When Kai saw the area, he said, "This is it."

We were both excited about spending every summer here, but the first year we came, it was winter. The Germans have strong traditions around Christmas, but I didn't grow up like that in S.A., where it's summer at Christmastime. I suggested we stray from tradition and stay in Portugal. That year we did and we had a different Christmas.

In the beginning, I was not living here full-time, but at the end of my third winter, we found an apartment to rent year-round and I furnished it. My next priority was to learn Portuguese, which kept me here a year. I studied at a school in Cascais, though I went back to Hamburg over the summer.

Nowadays, I live between two worlds, Germany and Portugal. My son has launched and lives with a friend in Hamburg. Because of my experiences as a backpacker in Europe, I encourage young people my son's age to travel, to just go. Travel broadens your horizons! Kai lives mainly in Hamburg and while he's still working, he comes when he can. We have grown apart, although we decided not to divorce.

Living in Portugal most of the year, I do feel as though I'm connecting with my father's roots. When Kai and I were in Lisbon that first time, he looked at me and he said, "I can now see where you've come from." The longer I live here, the more I feel as though my heritage is in my DNA. I can see and relate to my father here. There's no way for me to trace his family, but at times I'm aware that I could have relatives around the corner. Unfortunately, I will never know.

I realize I'm here, not just for me, but also for my father. I think he'd be proud. It's tragic that he had a chip on his shoulders about being half Portuguese. The Portuguese are such nice people, I see my father in them, and this is why

I'm also very motivated to learn the Portuguese language. I'm doing it for him.

Where is she now?

Rosemary is still dividing her time between Portugal and Germany, but now that she has set up a business in Cascais, she is here more often. Her business evolved out of her love of hiking trails in the area around where she lives. She offers three different scenic car trips or eight-guided hikes either along the coast or inland, and she also offers lots of insider tips along the way. *www.my-cascais.com*

Jayne Dyer

Introducing Jayne

Jayne brings conviviality to all her interactions. I noticed this when we were introduced at a gathering before a dance performance in Lisbon. She's also from Melbourne, Australia and thus I hoped to get to know her; since arriving in Portugal I'd met only one other person from the city where I'd spent my young adult years. Over the next 18 months there were many opportunities for get-togethers and conversations and that's when it became apparant to me that Jayne is an academic of art theory. What she tended to circumvent in those erudite conversations is the recognition she has received both for her pedagogical contributions and as an international cross-media artist. In 2005, Jayne was awarded a Commonwealth of Australia public service medal for contributions to arts and education; and in 2013 the Australian Federal Government awarded Jayne the inaugural Individual Artist Award for arts achievement in Asia.

In her words

My eldest sister remembers my mother Maimie as domestic, in a family oriented 1950s way. My memories are different, probably as I was so much younger, and my mother's life had changed. I recall her having many lovers and taking on extreme situations and jobs to survive. I followed in the slipstream.

My mother and her husband Tom were hoteliers. When I was born they had a bar in "the block" a cultural hub in central Melbourne, close to Her Majesty's Theater. Its bohemian atmosphere attracted a diverse crowd: theatergoers, actors, writers, musicians, prostitutes, politicians and transvestites. Maimie, who was a Betty Davis lookalike, gravitated towards the unconventional, adored costume, and would willingly mix with clients to experiment with the latest in theater makeup. I especially loved her long elbow length, green satin gloves with buttons at the wrist, unbuttoned when she languidly smoked a cigarette.

I am the youngest of five. There is a 17-year age gap between my eldest twin sisters and me. Almost a generation! By the time I was eight, my siblings had fled the nest. I think my mother felt liberated. She left Tom, who wasn't my biological father. Maimie had had an affair with Ernesto, a close family friend, and my father. Tom knew about the affair. Maimie would take me to her Italian lover's home on weekends. Ernesto kept a bedroom with "Jayne" printed on the door. This was the early '60s in Australia, and my mother was a trailblazer in the way she chose to live her life.

Ernesto wanted to marry Maimie, but once she was no longer with Tom, she chose not to be with Ernesto who eventually married another woman and had two more children. When I was 18, my sister encouraged me to delve into my Italian history – Ernesto had emigrated from Rome in the late 1940s – but it was not something I was ready or needed to do emotionally. I think there are some family stories that are better left intact, the insistent need to unpick can erase the essential intimacy and integrity of a situation. Nevertheless, Europeans assume I'm Italian.

It's an odd thing now living in southern Europe. It makes sense to me, my unexplained heartfelt link with this part of the world.

Maimie and I lived a nomadic life. It was a childhood with many adventures. I attended sixteen metropolitan and regional schools; at one point I missed school for six months. I was a loner, an isolated and very shy child. Each school offered sanctuaries: the library and the art room, my emotional, physical and intellectual cores. We rarely stayed anywhere for more than six months. Crazy, peripatetic, unstable, yes, yet in retrospect, I see I gained an emergent sense of self-containment and strength.

A young female teacher triggered a pivotal turning point in my life. I was in Year 10 in a less than stimulating school that praised typing skills over debating ability. This courageous woman recommended I change schools and clandestinely enrolled me in Elwood High School. Heaven! Suddenly it was okay to embrace a scholastic life, to be non-convergent, and, as a result of being amongst fellow achievers, my self-worth blossomed and instilled in me a love of education. In fact, education became my "way out" and my "way in" – the means to build a self-governed future.

I was determined to study visual art. In Australia it was a politically good time to have no family money as the Whitlam government policy of educational equity offered scholarships for tertiary studies. An undergraduate degree in Fine Arts from Melbourne University, and a Master of Arts from Royal Melbourne Institute of Technology University clarified my direction as an artist and academic. A chance meeting led to an interview for an academic position at Monash University in Melbourne. I got the job and found my feet.

At 24 I married my best friend. The day I married, I realized we were more like brother and sister and I'd wed his family. They had this great sense of camaraderie that I adored. I felt so included. Within a year I had left the marriage but kept the friendship.

Love – such a loaded word. As a young woman I was so appreciative if someone wanted me. By my 30s I realized this story needed revision as I'd meet lovely men and leave them. Or I'd meet men who wanted children, a wrong match for me, as I've never experienced that "loud ticking biological clock" of wanting a child. Again I'd move on. At 35 I met someone special. We were both in other relationships. Getting together caused enormous havoc. The relationship was on and off for years, eventually transforming into a dear love then to a lasting friendship; and ironically his children are now my family.

In my early career as an academic I eschewed opportunities to exhibit, as I didn't feel I had identified my voice as an artist. My vulnerable spot. I jumped into advocacy for visual arts equity in university programming. Realizing that the individual can contribute as an agent of change in course development and implementation, I was stimulated by the collaborative nature of learning that activates both the student and lecturer, and with my limited experience I was privileged to write for educational journals. And really, I found that period incredibly exciting. But my primary voice as an artist kept prodding me ...

With time came the confidence to exhibit my artwork and apply for arts funding. And by applying some of the skills from my academic career into my art practice, the "path of the artist" opened. I was first a painter, and my minimal non-figurative paintings were well received. But there was a *but* ... I was uneasy putting paint on a flat surface, uncomfortable making aesthetically oriented works, and far more excited by the stories people tell, and to discover ways an artist can engage with global issues through personal exchanges. This at a time when artists were emerging as cross-discipline performers, filmmakers and object makers, interacting in world issues, politics and society; all of which supported my natural tendencies. My art practice was not refuted, but rather, it was of its time.

Funding is a central issue for artists. Unlike salaried workers, artists are self-employed and incomes generated from sales of artwork or public and corporate commissions are erratic. Australian government cultural funding and private sponsorship to support artists' research and exhibitions overseas is competitive. I have been fortunate to develop projects in Asia, and more recently west Asia and Europe with support from Australian and international funding bodies.

The university system in Australia afforded me many opportunities to travel abroad. The usual arts and educational research, conferences, artist residencies, exhibitions and commissions have generally driven my travel focus. In the early 1980s, Australia was still culturally identified with the U.K. and Europe. I have had a deep, long-term relationship with Asia, in particular China, Taiwan and India. These countries, their geographic closeness to Australia, position Australia as an integral part of the Asian diaspora. Since the 1850s, Victorian gold rush Asian immigrants have expanded and enriched the Australian demography and changed Australian culture and education.

In 1992, not long after the Tiananmen Square demonstrations, I was invited to participate and attend an Australian initiative in Beijing. Two artists, an arts writer and curator accompanied the exhibition. It was my first time in China, and my first exhibition overseas. I was in Beijing for a month and though I'd been in other Asian countries before – Laos, Cambodia, Indonesia, Singapore, Taiwan, Malaysia, India – I was overwhelmed by the still palpable closed-door-Mao-dictatorship heritage. I'd never experienced illegal undercover pop-up exhibitions – raw, dislocated voices of artists responding to Tiananmen and opening up to a Western audience.

One night I was passed a scrap of paper with an address written in Mandarin. I found the small hutong alley and knocked on a door. Inside a woman lay naked in a bath of blood and pigs wandered aimlessly from room to room. I experienced a compelling strange connect/disconnect as a result of not being able to fully understand. During that month, I met a community of dissident artists, curators and writers. I returned to Beijing the following year supported by an Australia / Asia link artist residency grant. This was the start of an on-going conversation that culminated in moving to Beijing eleven years ago.

In 2007, I was commissioned to undertake a public artwork for K11 Art Foundation in Hong Kong. It made sense to create the work in Beijing, where I had a great community of mates, and ship it to Hong Kong. I packed two suitcases, planning to be in Beijing for a year, but I stayed. In fact, I haven't been back to live in Australia.

Colleagues in Australia counseled me to carefully consider my choice of stepping away from my university career, which by then was established in Sydney. I was resolute in my decision to leave. I've always left jobs, believing that I can only contribute so much, and to be honest, I get restless. Wages have never been a determinant for me. Experience has. An example: at 33 I received academic tenure at Monash University. An older colleague with tenure, said with excitement, "Now you'll be here all your life and be secure." Four years later I left.

I lived in Beijing for eight years. A city of then 23 million people enclosed in seven ring roads, each ring and its east, west, north, south orientation offering its own character. After the first year I was contacted by the Central Academy of Fine Art requesting that I establish an international visual arts program to introduce Chinese students to western models of learning. A 12-month program in which students would work with local and international practitioners in painting, sculpture, architecture, design, drawing, in preparation for graduate programs overseas. I thought what a rare opportunity to step inside the "China machine" to understand how things worked.

I headed up the program and couldn't believe the bureaucratic top-down control. It was probably the hardest, toughest work I've ever done! It made me acutely aware of how every culture has its ethical and achievement tenets. Certainly within the culture of the Australian university system I understood the ideology, but as an outsider in China, trying to understand the cultural system, it was extremely challenging.

In 2014, I took 58 international flights for art projects. Nine months in the air. Exciting, but also a bit loco. I needed an anchor somewhere. I own a place in Australia, familiar, warm, a good place where I have good friends. But there's another *but* ... Imagine wearing a big fluffy coat with no prickles ... I like something that jabs me a bit, that keeps me awake.

For me to continue to live in China had become off-limits politically and environmentally. I considered Istanbul – the collision of east and west is very exciting. Then synchronicity struck! In 2013 I visited Lisbon. One of my favorite relatives was attending the year long Maumaus Independent Study Program that speculates a central concern I value: "*How does an art school respond to the current state of political restlessness in an era of advanced capitalism and globalized methods of cultural production?*"

Visiting him I found Lisbon an uneasy time capsule of old, glorious Europe racing into the mid-21st century. And a geographical phenomenon that raises questions about our perception of what constitutes identity – Portugal's eastern border is Europe; its Atlantic border is Africa. In negotiating nationhood the Portuguese "gaze out" (to disparate implicated political histories) while Australians "look up" (to the rest of the world).

Now as an immigrant in Portugal, I am given a certain liberty to exist here, which is not necessarily the case in other countries where I've spent significant time. As an artist I can work anywhere, but for me, it is where one feels a sensibility to live that's important, and it is here. I subsequently bought an apartment and in 2015 made it home.

The idea of family means a lot to me, as do personal intimate friendships. In the past, in order to feel secure, I might have wanted conventional relationships. Now I revel in the lens through which I see my life – living alone but with a broad community of family, friends, and a creative network that does not adhere to expected behavioral roles. It all mishmashes together in a way that works for me. I have found a sense of calm in Portugal, with the knowledge that nothing is ever fixed. It's a mutable life, and in that sense, has an inherently unknowable future.

Where is she now?

Jayne continues to travel regularly, particularly within Europe for exhibitions, project development and collaborative artist residencies. Her recent project, *A perfect day* was a part of the 2018 Triennial of Photography at the Museum für Völkerkunde, Hamburg. The Triennial, titled *Breaking Point*, brought together artists from Europe, Asia, U.S.A., and the Middle East to stimulate the discussion on sustainable cultures and environmental issues. She is currently researching a new project for the May 2019 Porto Bienal at the Palácio de Cristal. The Biennale theme *Adaption and Transition* addresses our global uncertainty in relation to ecological and social behaviors. She lives in Lisbon and has a studio at Hangar Centro de Investigação Artistica in Graça. *www.jaynedyer.com*

Terri Blakley

Introducing Terri

Terri has recently started to color her short silver hair with streaks of pink and Caribbean blue. It's fun, kinda zany, and totally different, just like Terri. I don't see too many Portuguese women coloring their hair in this fashion but nevertheless Terri fits right in because she's fluent in both the language and the culture. Whenever I spend time with her out and about, she chats it up with everyone, and they with her. Having two dogs by her side helps as dogs always seem to be a talking point: kids love to pet them, adults often love to too, and inevitably a conversation ensues. I learn a lot watching Terri, she knows how to break down cultural barriers simply by being herself so that suddenly there's banter, laughter and snorting, and a multitude of *beijinhos*. "How did you do that?" I'll say bemused. "What?" she'll say, genuinely confused and obviously unaware of her capacity to communicate and engage the reserved Portuguese.

In her words

When I was growing up we lived seven miles from the Mexican border in Southern California. At age 17 we'd go over to dance, and for the drinks, which were really cheap. The age to cross from the U.S. into Mexico, unaccompanied by an adult, was 18. My mother would write a note to the border police saying, "Please allow my daughter to cross the border." When I was older we'd often go to Tijuana for shopping, for lunch, for concerts. My first travel experience was to Disneyland in 1955 when I was four. It had just opened.

By the time I was 19, I was in junior college in Chula Vista, south of San Diego. One of the classes I took was Spanish. I didn't know it at the time, but my teacher was from Portugal. It was later, when I started studying the language that I realized the spelling of his name was Portuguese.

I continued to study Spanish, taking it to level 3. When I went to the University of California (UC) at Santa Barbara, where I was required to choose a major, the only thing I really liked enough was Spanish, so I declared it as my major. I had no idea how difficult it would be, all that literature, even pre-Columbian literature! Oh boy, it was one of those things that if I'd had a clue of the challenges ahead, I might not have done it, but I did, and I loved it.

In 1974, I graduated from UC Santa Barbara majoring in Spanish. I got a job as a bilingual welfare worker in San Diego, later working as the Principal's Secretary at a high school. During the high school's 1977 summer break, I attended a two-week cultural and linguistic school in Mexico. I stayed with a family, and they introduced me to a Brazilian singer's records in both Spanish and Portuguese. This was my first exposure to Roberto Carlos. I credit my love of his music as one of the reasons I decided to study Portuguese. I wanted to understand the lyrics and what he was singing about, I just loved how it sounded.

I didn't really want to keep working at the high school. What I really wanted was to go back to school and continue studying. So in January of 1978, I enrolled to study Brazilian

Portuguese, taking a couple of other Spanish classes too, at San Diego State University. That was the year I met Mark, whom I would marry three years later. We were in Portuguese 101 together. Around that time, a group of us went over the border to Tijuana to see Roberto Carlos in concert. Mark also fell in love with his music. We still listen to his songs today.

During my second semester, in September of 1978, Portugal's Naval training "tall ship," The Sagres, came to San Diego. The reason may have been the big Portuguese community in San Diego – tuna fishermen from the Açores mostly. Someone contacted our Portuguese professor and said, "Are there any students that would like to come down and be cultural liaisons with the guys on the ship?" We were studying *Brazilian* Portuguese, so nobody was interested, but my friend and I volunteered.

We went down to the ship and the officers invited us on board and we had a blast. We also took them to some cultural sites around San Diego and in return the officers invited us to dinner each night on the ship. One of the guys I met on board, a marine by the name of Ramiro, said to me, "If you come to Portugal, here's my sister's phone number. Her name is Mila and you could stay with her."

While finishing my studies at San Diego State, I tutored English as a Second Language (ESL), mostly to Japanese and Saudi students and Algerians too. I realized I really wanted to get a Master's in Foreign Language Education instead of Latin American Studies.

The first time I traveled overseas was July 1979. My girl-friend was married to a guy from England and that year she graduated from San Diego State. Her in-laws came out from the U.K. I met them and they invited me to come and stay on their farm.

At much the same time that I received the invitation to go to England, I'd also applied for a scholarship with the Gulbenkian Foundation in Lisbon to study Portuguese at a summer program. I hadn't heard back, so I went ahead and bought my ticket to England. At the last minute I heard from the Gulbenkian, but they weren't giving fellowships that year.

I went to England on my own and had a good time and from London I took the train to Lisbon. I had no idea what I was doing, plus it was August and the train was really crowded and hot. Luckily there were some German guys on the train and they helped me figure out where to get on and off and they helped me carry all my gear. I loved seeing the people who lived in houses along the train lines. Their job was to come out and wave the flag or a lamp at night as the train went by, unlike today with the modern "bing, bing, bing" at the train crossings.

When I arrived in Lisbon, I called Ramiro's sister, Mila, who was recently divorced. We'd never met but she and her two kids and a friend came and picked me up and I ended up staying with her for three weeks. As it turned out, Mila is the same age as my sister, they're only 18 days apart, and when we first met I was 28, her kids were 7 and 10 and now the kids are in their 40s, which gives you an idea of how old I am! Mila is still my best friend in Portugal today.

During those weeks staying with Mila, I was hanging out with her brother a lot. Apparently he thought we might get married, but I was already enrolled in the University of Texas (UT) to do my Master's degree and I was going back to that. While in Portugal, we had fun going to the beach, we went camping, and we went to the markets where I learned how to push in, instead of standing back and waiting my turn. I enjoyed it so much I hated to leave.

Back at UT, in September of 1979, I registered in Foreign Language Education specializing in TEFL (Teaching English as a Foreign Language) and I also took a part time job in the Zoology Department raising and caring for exotic cockroaches for experiments. After a month back at UT, I re-encountered Mark, who had disappeared for a year, but here he was at UT, and with a girlfriend, but we'd do things together sometimes. The Christmas of 1979 we drove back to San Diego together and in January he came to stay for several weeks and never left!

Mark took classes and worked as well. All the while, I was thinking that I could probably teach in Portugal. One of the first women I met at UT was Sandi, and her husband was Portuguese. She told me about the American Language Institute (ALI) in Lisbon.

After I graduated in May 1981, Mark and I got married, we moved back to San Diego with my two dogs, Buckwheat and Butterscotch, and for a time, I taught ESL, while Mark worked at a fish market in heavily Portuguese-inhabited Point Loma.

I had written to the ALI in Lisbon about a job and they sent me a letter saying that they would be interviewing in Los Angeles that April. I went ahead and interviewed and at the end the interviewer asked, "Do you have any questions?" I said, "Well yes, I have this husband, could he get some hours working in Lisbon too?" With my Master's I could get a contract, but Mark didn't have his Master's. However, there was a school in Lisbon related to the Royal Academy of the Arts, it was called the International School, and they had a month long intensive teacher-training course. Greg, the interviewer, said that if Mark passed that, he'd get some hours teaching. And that's what happened.

Mark and I, Buckwheat and Butterscotch, arrived in Lisbon in the summer of 1982 and we taught here until 1984. We loved it. However, even though I was a good teacher, I wasn't great at being a teacher. I'm too obsessive. I'd work 80 hours and teach 21 hours. Nevertheless, we met a lot of wonderful people and today we're still in touch with many of our former students.

Mark and I also taught classes at Carris, the bus company in Lisbon. There was no heat in the building and it was so cold in winter, we wore coats, gloves and hats to teach. For the last six months of 1984 we taught in Porto. Unfortunately, Mark's dad was dying, so in January 1985 we went back to San Diego.

My father-in-law died not long after our return and once Mark's family's affairs were sorted out, we decided to go back to Austin, Texas. Buckwheat had died in April 1984 in São Pedro do Estoril and Butterscotch had died in February of 1985 in San Diego. So before we went back to Austin, we got a new puppy that was a cross between a Cocker Spaniel and a Labrador Retriever and we named him Rowdy.

After the three of us got to Austin, I landed a job in the Spanish and Portuguese department at UT, and we ended up living there until December 1988. In the meantime, we adopted a red Cocker Spaniel, Amber, from friends and then we added Mafalda to our doggy family, a Portuguese water dog who was sent over from Portugal.

In the fall of 1987, we received a phone call from ALI, "Did we want to come back?" They needed teachers in Porto. Porto hadn't been as fun as Lisbon, but we said, "Yes." Just as we five were settling back in to life in Portugal, my mother got sick and six months later, in July of 1988, we returned to the States again, where we lived until 2014.

During the early days of our time in Portugal it was like living 50 years behind what we were used to in California. On my first trip I was in Rossio in Lisbon, I didn't know my way around, so in Brazilian Portuguese I asked a guy in a little shop for directions. When he responded, I had a hard time understanding him. Finally he just closed his shop and walked me over to where I wanted go.

People had time in those days, they'd stop and chat on the streets, it was a slow and gentle pace. Life happened in the cafes. Cafe culture was, and still is, part of the daily routine. There used to be much less car traffic, which meant the buses and trains were often packed. And you would never have seen women wearing pants, much less jeans, unless they were quite young. Women wore skirts. In that sense, it was old fashioned.

In the early days we couldn't find some things, basic things like say, the vegetable, celery. And no one seemed to know what we were talking about when we went looking for it. Of course you can get it now, but then you could only find very basic local produce such as potatoes, tomatoes, cabbage, lettuce, beans, etc., and everything was incredibly inexpensive. Portugal was a very poor country back then. We knew people who were receiving only 10 percent of their salary. There just wasn't the money to pay workers' salaries.

And there were the Portuguese returning from Africa after the colonial wars. Families who'd settled in Africa or who'd been born there were coming back with nothing! Once they returned, many were living in shacks in shantytowns, like the favelas of Brazil today. It was easy to see that many Portuguese were depressed. Life was simple but it was tough. There were those who'd lived under the dictatorship from 1933 until 1974, and during that time many people disappeared at the hands of the secret police.

Our American friend B and her family lived in Portugal during the 1974 Carnation Revolution that toppled the dictatorship. Mark met B when he was doing his teaching course in Lisbon at the International School. He came home from the first day and said, "I met a lady from Riverside, California." The three of us started to do things together.

B and her husband and their daughter who was 2, had moved to Portugal in the mid-1960s. Their second daughter was born here in '69. After the revolution, B's husband decided to move the family back to California but B wasn't happy with that. B's husband bought her an apartment in Portugal and she returned, put her girls in

Catholic School here, and her husband stayed in California. They remained married till he died, but she lived here and he lived in California.

They'd left the States in part because B is African American and her husband was Caucasian. They were in Los Angeles during a time of racial tension and social unrest that resulted in the Watts riots. They both worked for the Police Department and he was demoted for dating B, who was a subordinate and also, I'm guessing, because she's African American. They were thinking of moving to Ireland, but it was quite expensive, so B, with her 2-year-old in tow, came south searching and found Portugal, a small, clean, quiet and inexpensive country where there was no racial tension. They decided to move here.

When Mark and I were living in Lisbon, we'd come out to Cascais where B was living and take walks and do things together. After we went back to the States in 1988, B's daughter came to live with her dad. Their other daughter also lived in L.A. When B came to L.A. to visit, we'd get together. During her last few visits to California, we noticed she had dementia and it was progressing. In 2013, we went to India with her for about a month, at which point she was often very disoriented.

We decided to come back to Portugal ASAP, to help B out. I'd already retired, and we'd been planning that when Mark retired, we'd come back. The decision was easy. In fact, for years I used to have dreams that we were trying to get back to see Mila, my friend since my very first visit to Portugal, and that I could never get to her house. I would wake up crying! I'd have those dreams over and over during all those years. It was like coming home when we finally came back.

We moved with our two dogs, Buck and Chacha, on February 16, 2014, and our house that we found online, was a five-minute walk from B. Once settled, we took on the role of looking after her. We jokingly call Mark her "man servant" and I'm her "lady-in-waiting." We've noticed a continual decline in her cognitive function, but we do what we can, knowing that we also need to stay patient with her. It helps B and it helps her younger daughter, who lives in Spain with her husband and kids.

Something that has made life easier here is having connections, or *cunha*. It's all about *who you know* and making those connections has been aided by the fact that we speak Portuguese. We have a lot of Portuguese friends and we live in a Portuguese neighborhood and when we're out walking the dogs, we always chat with the neighbors. We have a real sense of community. We feel more involved here too, probably as a result of Mark and I doing more community work than we did in California.

We also have a lot of ex-pat friends, though there are no ex-pats in our neighborhood, but we go between both communities easily.

Despite experiencing some culture shock on my first visit, I've always felt comfortable in Portugal. It's as though this is where I should be. I've even felt at times that maybe I'd been Portuguese in a previous life. I don't how to explain that. It's just a feeling. Sometimes you can't put things like that into words. I do feel there was something predestined about my relationship with this country. Now we live in Cascais near the coast where we love to walk our dogs on the beach, and they love it too!

Where is she now?

Terri and her husband Mark and their dogs, Buck and Chacha, are still in Cascais, living and loving their retirement with one foot in their Portuguese neighborhood community, and one foot in the expat community. They volunteer for local dog rescue charities such as *Dogs of Portugal*, an all-volunteer group that devotes their time to improving the lives of and the chances of adoption for abandoned and mistreated dogs, and a dog rescue sanctuary in Setúbal called *Cantinho da Milu*. They're also involved with *Cascais Ambiente* and IWP *Friends of the Environment*, helping improve the conditions of local forests and ocean-side dunes.

Louise Ross

In her words
In one of the indigenous Koori languages of Australia, Korumburra means *blowfly*. It's also a very small town nestled in a rural area of undulating green hills two-hours southeast of Melbourne, and it's where I grew up in the 1960s with my sister and my parents, who had a very happy and traditional marriage.

My mother had been a fashion designer in 1950s Melbourne. She used to tell my sister and me a story that began like this: "When I met your father and married, I gave up my career to move to the countryside to have a family." It was a bittersweet story, laced with loss for a life unlived. Until, toward the end of her life, a writer contacted her with a request to interview her about her work as a custom designer with a fashion house in the epicenter of Melbourne's rag trade. Details of Mum's career were recorded for the purpose of developing the protagonist, Tilly Dunnage, in the revenge-comedy novel, *The Dressmaker*, which was adapted for the screen and starred Kate Winslet.

Dad, who was 11 years older than Mum, had his own stories, which he recorded on a Dictaphone. Duplicate CDs of those recordings were distributed to various family members. I particularly loved listening to the story of his first kiss. As a teen, he'd been sent to Nouméa, the capital of the South Pacific archipelago New Caledonia, to improve his spoken French, and there he'd met a young girl with garlicky breath the likes of which he hoped he'd never encounter again! When aged 12, I holidayed in Nouméa with my parents, Dad's excellent French came in handy, and I loved all the garlicky Creole food.

My father was an only child and his parents divorced when he was 10. He lived with his mother and saw his father on school holidays. Sadly, when Dad was 20 and at an Australian army training facility, he was notified of his father's death from a burst appendix. Not long after, he set sail for the Middle East where he was on the front line in the Western Desert, commanding his regiment to "FIRE" their canons into Rommel's German trenches. Later he was sent to fight the Japanese in New Guinea. Mum used to say that in the early days of their marriage, he was still rolling out of and under the bed at sudden loud sounds. We all lived with his post-traumatic stress; so did he, till the ripe old age of 93.

Before he died, we learned from a cousin, who had researched their family ancestry, that Dad's mother's forebears, Jewish shopkeepers in Sheerness, England, were convicted of hiring burglars in 1819 to repossess unpaid goods. The Solomon brothers were subsequently sent to Van Diemen's Land, the name given to the penal colony on Australia's island state of Tasmania. They worked in Hobart as assigned convicts until, as freemen, they built up their own businesses. As their success and prominence grew, one of the Solomon brothers built Hobart's synagogue, now the oldest remaining synagogue in Australia.

Dad was incurious about all this, but the year after his death, my sister and I, keen to learn more, visited Hobart and the Jewish temple built by our ancestor. In contrast, we learned a lot about our maternal heritage via our mother's mother. Nicknamed "The Duchess," she loved to hold court at family gatherings and tell the story of crossing the Nullarbor Desert with my grandfather, and their four children (my mother was number three), in a 1920s-style jalopy, embellishing the journey of their 3,400 km Perth-to-Melbourne migration with every re-telling.

Both my parents were great readers, conversationalists and grammarians. Mealtimes were opportunities for discussions and we were expected to participate. My father considered an education the most important thing he could give his daughters and it was standard practice in rural communities to send children to boarding school if you could afford to. After two years at the local rural high school, my sister and I went to boarding school in Melbourne. Leaving the comfort and security of home at 13 was hard; I missed my parents and my own bedroom. However I was determined to be courageous, strong and adaptable.

I was a very shy and insecure teen, but I had an extremely strong will which benefited me when making decisions about my life's direction. My first big decision was to take a gap year after secondary school, to explore the 'next step'. Instead of university, that year I decided on culinary school, encouraged by Mum's comment: "Wherever you go, people have to eat!" After working through my certificate degree at a small woman-owned catering company, followed by second-chef'ing with Melbourne's doyen caterer, where we cooked for A-list clients, I took my culinary talents abroad. I was 22.

My contemporaries were all heading to Europe, rendezvous-ing to backpack and travel together. I chose to go it alone and head to the U.S. My first stop was New York. My parents' concerns about this were not entirely unfounded. I saw things on the streets and subways of 1982 New York that I'd only ever seen on TV and in the movies. Unconcealed weapons, open drug use, and homelessness: kids my own age sleeping on the streets and shooting up. In an ice-cream parlor, with *36 flavors*, a wannabe Broadway actor tap-danced atop the tables while I ordered my double-cone. The distraction gave someone the chance to pickpocket my backpack and I lost all my money. Not easy experiences, but they wised and toughened me up.

I spent three months in the U.S. traveling around on Greyhound buses, crossing into Canada and going as far south as Mexico before heading to London where I ran the kitchen of a small private hotel on Hampstead Heath. But my sole intention in London was to find a winter job in one of Europe's ski resorts.

An independently owned, small British ski company with six chalets in Courcheval, France, took me on. A couple of months later the team of a dozen young employees, including one other Australian and me, drove in convoy from North London to Dover, where we caught the ferry to Calais and drove across France and up into the Alps, arriving in Courcheval early November before the season started.

I loved to ski. It had been my outdoor passion from age 18 when my first love introduced me to the exhilarating sport. In Australia I'd worked at one ski resort during my gap year, and then another when I'd finished my culinary degree. The rhythm of shifting one's weight from side to side, while zooming down a mountain, felt to me like flying.

The guests at my 18-bed chalet in Courcheval were groups of French and British. The French were the most complimentary of my cooking, but well into the season it was a British guest who suggested I should write a cookbook. Twenty-eight years later, during the emergent "celebrity chef" era, I did just that.

What I discovered about myself during the ski season, particularly when sitting down to dinner with the chalet guests, was that my ability to contribute to bigger conversations was wanting. I'd dedicated time and energy to building my skill as a chef, labor-intensive and creative work, but it was never going to be an intellectually challenging vocation. I concluded it was time to go back to school.

At 24, I enrolled as a mature-age student in a BA program at an Institute of Technology in Melbourne. My focus was psychology and philosophy, but very soon I was bored witless. My extra-curriculum reading, however, was not boring, as I'd discovered the works of Swiss psychiatrist, Carl Jung. At the end of my second year, one of my class mates and I applied for student working visas so we could work in the U.S. for our summer break, the winter season in the northern hemisphere. We chose Park City, a ski resort in Utah. Apparently it had some of the best powder!

Early in the season, while strolling though the village, I ran into an Australian friend, someone I'd met in Courcheval. A 'ski and surf bum', Wayne was an avid consumer of New Age literature. He lent me some books, including Marilyn Ferguson's epoch-making *The Aquarian Conspiracy* in which she explores her theory on personal and social transformation. On the book's resource page a list of American colleges with graduate programs on this topic caught my eye. I called those colleges, requesting their school prospectuses. Several months later, and back in Australia, I deferred indefinitely from my studies, and applied to the colleges in the U.S. I was accepted into a small graduate school in Boulder, Colorado to study Jungian Psychology, with an emphasis on dream analysis.

At 26 I left Australia again for the U.S. This time, I was leaving with no sense of when, or if, I'd return.

Boulder is nestled up against the foothills of the Rocky Mountains and in 1986 it was a university town in economic recession. With a stagnant economy, there wasn't much happening. But a lot was going on for me! My studies encouraged endless self-examination via experiential classes and compulsory psychotherapy with a therapist in the field of my research. Thirty years on, I still consult with the same Jungian dream therapist, a woman who has become like a wise older sister and mentor to me.

With all that inner work came personal growth and transformation. In my outer world, I met and married my husband. We were 28. A year later I submitted my first significant piece of writing, my Master's thesis, thereby earning a BA/MA in Jungian Psychology and Counseling. After graduating and building a small private practice as a psychotherapist, I simultaneously worked in a women's clinic for three years as a counselor, later writing a collection of 45 short stories about the experience. It didn't get published. No matter, there was plenty of encouragement from my peers to try my hand at other projects, once I'd resigned from the clinic work.

What I loved about living in the U.S. was the emotional and creative freedom to *live your best life* (an Oprah adage) without the discouragement of being diminished for one's achievements, the "Tall Poppy Syndrome" so prevalent in Australian culture. I set about making the most of that freedom.

In the early '90s my husband and I went into partnership with my sister and her husband in Australia. They were manufacturing outdoor clothing in a factory outside Melbourne and exporting it to the U.S. and Europe. We were the U.S. distribution office. My role was part-time office support, which gave me my own time to launch and operate a Sunday outdoor art and craft market over the summers; facilitate dream-analysis groups; and design and co-facilitate with a friend workshops on *Dressing Authentically*; followed by promoting myself to women in small businesses as a personal and professional development consultant.

All these opportunities in my 30s were marvelous, challenging, and character building. The most difficult of those experiences was the end of my marriage at 38. Scott and I had traveled well when we went abroad, to Australia and Europe, including a road trip through Spain in 1994 that ended with several magical days on the beach in southern Portugal! But that seemed to be the only time we got along, when we removed ourselves from the self-imposed limitations of domesticity and a conventional marriage.

My parents expected that I'd return to Australia when I divorced. What they failed to consider is that from my mid-20s, I'd steadily built a life for myself in the U.S., and though I didn't love the extreme climate at altitude – Boulder is a mile above sea level – I had community and friends and the creative freedom to *live my best life*, and I wasn't about to give that up.

After my divorce, I worked as a promotions coordinator at a preparatory school for mature-age international students from developing countries. Their governments were funding their graduate and post-graduate studies in business and economics, but before entering U.S. colleges, the students first needed to acculturate into American life and social practices, while also improving their English. In promotional materials, I called the school a "mini United Nations," a term I also use in the introduction to this book.

Just shy of my 40th birthday, I was retrenched from that job. A huge disappointment as I loved the students with their culturally diverse stories, and my colleagues, all of whom had lived and worked internationally. Quickly I picked up a mediation contract and consulting work with technology companies that were expanding in the now burgeoning entrepreneurial community of Boulder and Denver. Then in 2000 the dot-com crash occurred, and the consulting work dried up.

On the side in a monthly writing group, I'd been developing a comic fictional character, 39-year-old Tildy Wilson. With sporadic work only, and time on my hands, I decided to write Tildy into a rom-com novel. Nine months later, and with only a rough first draft, a screenwriter and producer in Boulder expressed interest in optioning the novel. With no clue about the film industry, or the ins and outs of having an unpublished manuscript optioned for the screen, I responded, "Maybe, but I need to understand what this might mean." Over the next 12 years, with a

sequel completed, and a business built up around Tildy,
I learned an enormous amount about the industry in
particular that everyone says, "Yes" until they change their
mind and say, "No."

The business I created was branded with a colorful and cheeky
illustrated image of Tildy. The products included two novels,
the first, I self-published and the sequel, I pitched to literary
agents. There was a blog on best girlfriend wisdom written
in Tildy's voice, and a website with a store that sold spin-off
merchandise that I had made in China after a whirlwind
3-week trip visiting factories in Shanghai, Guangzhou,
Shenzhen and Hong Kong. And there was a huge outlay of
money! Foolishly, I'd invested mostly my money to create a
dream too big for me to make real. The business imploded
several years after it was launched.

Nevertheless, I kept at it. In 2007, I signed on with a literary
agent who believed she could sell my sequel. Six months later
she dropped me, saying another client was taking up all of
her time. I learned the other client was John Travolta, and
Susan was in the process of selling his memoir. Not to be
deterred I pitched other agents, actresses with production
companies, and Hollywood bigwigs, determined to sell Tildy
in all her manifestations: the sequel, a film concept, a TV
concept, and comedy sketches. There was always interest
… until the interest turned to, "No."

A man I met, a lawyer who'd helped clear up all my Tildy
business dealings, encouraged me to start writing a blog about
my other love: food. It was 2008 and the global economic
crash was in full swing. Suddenly people had less dispos-
able income to spend on eating out, and less to spend at

the grocery store. The timing was perfect for me to launch my book on shopping responsibly, and cooking and eating well on a budget. Steve, my agent, called me one day saying, "This cookbook concept is great Louise, but I can't sell it, the publishers want a rock-star celebrity chef!"

When my father died in 2010 – Mum had died seven years earlier – it was a natural transition into the next stage of life. A sobering chapter that had me standing on the precipice of 50 looking back at what had been, while wondering what next?

In 2011, I took myself to Mexico for a weeklong workshop and met a Portuguese woman. We became great friends. Over the next two years, Maria João visited me in Colorado and I visited her. On each trip to Lisbon her family, extended family, and family friends, most of whom had lived in Mozambique during the Salazar years, were incredibly welcoming and generous, introducing me to their language, food, culture, and life in Portugal. I was absolutely captivated.

From 2010 onwards, I had been spending so much time traveling outside the U.S. it occurred to me that my residency might be in jeopardy. Consulting with a professional in 2013, I discovered that that was not the case, but after some discussion the attorney commented, "It sounds to me as if you're considering moving abroad." She was right. Ten months later, I sold my apartment in Boulder and moved to a residence on the doorstep of the Atlantic Ocean. Within a couple of weeks of arriving, I began Portuguese classes and within a month, I'd signed on as a member of IWP. A year later, I began interviewing women for this book.

Where is she now?

I'm still living in São João do Estoril and loving my life on the coast. I'm a Portuguese resident and I own real estate now, so I do feel quite settled and thus it's feasible that I could end up staying longer than I originally planned.

Afterword

Women who walk are 'blueprint breakers': women who either intentionally ditched the cultural norm of do well at school, graduate, get a job, settle down in one place, get married, have kids or they accidentally discarded those norms and wound up enjoying less conventional, peripatetic and international lives. We rightly celebrate these female 'blueprint breakers', who in the past were more likely to be stigmatized.

Each of us is a work in progress, often going through distinct periods of growth and consolidation. This process is accelerated when we take ourselves (or are taken) out of our comfort zone. Changing country and culture often ruptures our comfort zone, leaving us feeling exposed and vulnerable. We unconsciously attempt to use our internal cultural model to help us work out how to behave in the new culture. Without useful reference points, we're jettisoned into a phase of rapid learning, whereby we expand our internal cultural model, which can be exhausting and exhilarating in equal measure.

We update our life story according to our new reality and what's taken out or glossed over, what's left in and maybe embellished, shapes our identity. A strong sense of identity is useful in adverse or challenging circumstances because it encourages resilience – a common thread in *Women Who Walk*. Resilience in turn enhances one's sense of identity. The ways in which the 20 women in this book boost their resilience is varied, for some it's their partner or family that makes the difference, for others their work or community.

There are seven elements that contribute to our resilience: partner; family; friends; community; work; skills and money. We only need three to feel strong and resilient at any given time. When we move country many of these elements instantly weaken – often we've left behind our friends and our extended family – and in the new country, we haven't had time yet to build a new community around us and we may not have a job and are living off our savings. No wonder that after the initial 'honeymoon' period of the new country and culture is over, we don't feel very resilient at all.

The single biggest predictor of success in any relocation is agency: the belief that you can influence your future. For aspiring or struggling expatriates the prevailing message in *Women Who Walk* is take action, be the director of your life story – it may help to record your story, to tell it, to edit it. Just as important is to connect with others and find your tribe, make things happen, learn new skills and strengthen the belief that you steer your life.

Absorb, then apply, the 20 redemptive narratives of *Women Who Walk* rich with stories of growing self-reliance, expanded identity, valuable lessons learned, insights gleaned, and then make your own unique blueprint for life, wherever you're living right now.

Alison Collis – Psychotherapist
www.alisoncollis.com

Acknowledgments

Immersing oneself in another person's life story is a journey in itself, a privileged and intimate journey of discovery that always surprises and delights. I am deeply grateful to the women whose stories appear in this book, who collaborated with me on this project, granting me permission to travel with them into their world. I would also like to thank the women whose stories are not included. Their stories, nonetheless, helped inform and develop the project.

To *International Women in Portugal* thank goodness the club exists to help expatriate women "feel at home in this beautiful country" because without my active involvement as a member and volunteer *Women Who Walk* would not exist! Thank you IWP for creating such a welcoming, rich and diverse international environment in which to socialize, connect, listen and learn as well as make wonderful women friends.

Special thanks to Diana Lourenco Hill for suggesting that I bookend each story; Cheryl Meechan, my early reader, for your honest feedback; Jayne Dyer for your wisdom and insightful content editing; Alison Collis for agreeing to write the Afterword; Leonie Yeates for your eagle eye as the copy editor; David Cronin for your stellar professional support designing and laying out the book; Christina and Michael Hultén for your front-cover design; Peta Burchell and Terri Blakley for proofreading the galley;

and to the ever pragmatic Marion Roach Smith, memoir writer, coach, and editor, who helped me advance a sliver of an idea into something I feel proud of.

Resources

If you're reading this book because you're curious to learn more about living in Portugal, you might find helpful the following list of resources that are available to the international community in Lisbon and along the Linha.

This is by no means a complete list. With further online research, readers will discover additional clubs, resources, websites and Facebook pages.

International Women In Portugal (IWP)
https://www.iwpportugal.org

Americans Living in Portugal
https://www.americansinportugal.org

Royal British Club (RBC)
http://www.royalbritishclub.pt/en-gb.aspx

British Community Council (BCC)
https://www.bcclisbon.org

Women's Royal Voluntary Service (WRVS)
www.facebook.com/WRVSLisbon

The Swedish Club
http://portugal.swea.org

South Africans Living in Portugal
https://www.facebook.com/SouthAfricansLivingInPortugal

SmartExpat (Formely the online magazine AngloInfo)
https://smartexpat.com/portugal/lisbon

InterNations
https://www.internations.org

PortugalConnexions
https://www.portugalconnexions.com/home

Meetup Lisbon
www.meetup.com/cities/pt/lisbon/

ExpatFocus
https://www.expatfocus.com

Facebook pages
   The Drop-in Chit Chat Café Portugal (Ad Free)
   Expats in Portugal
   ~~~ Expat in Portugal ~~~
   ~ Americans in Portugal ~ The Expats Group ~
   Americans Expat in Portugal
   International Friends Lisbon
   Lisbon International – Accommodation
   Expats Cascais
   Expats World Lisbon
   IWP Members Forum
   What's on in Cascais, Lisbon, Sintra?
   Local Services & News in Cascais / Sintra
   Job Opportunities Cascais
   Americans & FriendsPT

Book Group Discussion Questions

1. Which stories resonated most strongly with you? Why?

2. What compelled the women in these stories to leave their home country? What compelled you to leave ... or to stay?

3. Is it possible to feel like an outsider in your own country?

4. What are the differences and or similarities of moving within your country versus moving to another country?

5. What are some of the challenges you faced in leaving your home state / county or country? Language? Culture? Economics? Lifestyle?

6. On page 145, one of the interviewee says, "If we internationals were to go back to the countries where we're from ..." And then she pauses for a moment, and continues with "actually, I don't believe in going back." What is your response to this comment?

7. What does "home" mean to you? Where is your home?

8. Two of the interviewees are Adult Third Culture Kids: people raised in a culture other than their parents or born of parents from two different cultures and then raised in a third culture other than that of their parents. Are you an Adult Third Culture Kid? If so, what do

you perceive as the advantages and disadvantages to being an Adult Third Culture Kid.

9. Several women talk about being drawn to or inexplicably pulled to Portugal (which could be any country or city around the world). Have you had this experience? If so, to where, and what was the pull?

10. Several of the interviewees are "trailing spouses" a term that has been coined to describe women (and men) who follow their spouse around the world to various job postings. Are you a trailing spouse? If so, how do you feel about that moniker? And what has the 'trailing' experience been like for you?

11. There are two quotes at the beginning of Women Who Walk. When you think about why you left your country, which of these 2 quotes do you most identify with and why?

12. Do the interviewee's stories inspire you? If so in what way?

Made in the USA
Lexington, KY
19 July 2019